BEYOND DIVERSITY

ADVANCE PRAISE:

"As a Black woman I have long advocated for organizations to address the systemic racism that Black and Brown people struggle with every day. *Beyond Diversity* lifts the lid on how bias and privilege have benefitted the privileged few at the expense of the marginalized many. It provides a much-needed directive for those in power to get educated and use their influence to finally break down the barriers that have left so many of us behind."

—MINDA HARTS, Speaker, Founder, and Author of *The Memo*

"*Beyond Diversity* is an urgently needed, eminently practical book that every leader should read. Bhargava and Brown have taken on a tough topic with sharp minds and open hearts. In a dozen crisp and fascinating chapters, they show how to move past mere sentiment to bring genuine inclusion into action."

—DANIEL H. PINK, New York Times bestselling author
of *When, Drive,* and *To Sell Is Human*

"Successful women advocate for themselves. This wonderfully wide-ranging book offers a valuable look at the context of the world we all must live in today, and offers an eye-opening roadmap for how any of us can do that more effectively. For any woman of color seeking to unearth her individual power, this is an essential read."

—DEEPA PURUSHOTHAMAN, Author of *The First, The Few, The Only* and
Co-Founder of nFormation

"Thought-provoking, layered, and fresh. Each one of us has a part to play in creating a more inclusive world. Wherever you may be in your journey, *Beyond Diversity* is the weapon in your DEI arsenal. For the non-believers, bystanders, and uninitiated—be inspired to make better inclusion choices. For the believers, advocates, and experts—be rejuvenated in your fight for equity."

—MICHELLE KING, Author of *The Fix* and CEO of Equality Forward

"With this important contribution, Rohit Bhargava and Jennifer Brown invite everyone to see themselves in the diversity and inclusion conversation. *Beyond Diversity* provides a roadmap to help all of us step into the conversation, however imperfectly, and to learn to take action and be a part of the movement toward a more diverse, inclusive, and equitable society."

—ERIN URITUS, CEO of Out and Equal

"Really enjoyed this book! I loved the simple structure and use of storytelling to build empathy and understanding across all the different dimensions of diversity. *Beyond Diversity* is a must-read for anyone committed to a world where we all belong and contribute fully. Authors Jennifer Brown and Rohit Bhargava write with compassion and empathy, while giving us a little kick in the pants to get involved at the same time. The reality is, we can all do more to make our communities and workplaces more inclusive. This important book provides a pathway for making it happen."

—MICHELE MEYER-SHIPP, Chief People Officer for Major League Baseball

"Jennifer and Rohit have artfully used the power of storytelling to connect the reader with the lived experience of LGBTQ+ people and other marginalized communities that have been systemically discriminated against and 'othered' for far too long. We must build a society that is more inclusive of transgender and non-binary people and honors their contributions and realities. Their book opens eyes, hearts, and minds!"

—AMBER HIKES, Chief Equity and Inclusion Officer, American Civil Liberties Union (ACLU)

"To embrace change and create a more inclusive workplace, we must tackle demanding questions that diminish opportunities for minorities and underserved groups. It will take bold action and uncomfortable moments. Yet, in this new era of hope and resilience, we will collectively navigate endings and embrace new beginnings. Now, more than ever is time to dismiss old practices and pivot to real, sustainable change. The progress beyond these breakthroughs will create a generational impact."

—JORDAN BABINEAUX, Former NFL Player

"As a theoretical neuroscientist focused on the future of human potential, and the 'tax' so many of us pay on being different, this book educates the reader beautifully on what gets in the way of our ability to thrive. With real insights from real people, Brown and Bhargava document concrete ways we can together build the kind of world I want my kids to live in."

—**DR. VIVIENNE MING**, Founder & Executive Chair, Socos Labs

BEYOND DIVERSITY

IDEAPRESS
PUBLISHING

Printed in the United States.

Ideapress Publishing | www.ideapresspublishing.com

Cover Design: Amanda Hudson
Mosaic Art: Zharia Shinn
Cover Fonts: Trenda, LatinoType

Cataloging-in-Publication Data is on file with the Library of Congress.

ISBN: 978-1-64687-051-6

Special Sales
Ideapress Books are available at a special discount for bulk purchases for sales promotions and premiums, or for use in corporate training programs. Special editions, including personalized covers, a custom foreword, corporate imprints, and bonus content, are also available.

BEYOND DIVERSITY

12 Non-Obvious Ways To Build A More Inclusive World

ROHIT BHARGAVA
JENNIFER BROWN

With:

Andrius Alvarez-Backus, Chhavi Arya, Karen Dahms,
Sandhya Jain-Patel, Kaleena Sales, Monika Samtani

IDEAPRESS
PUBLISHING

WASHINGTON, D.C.

*For all the voices that chose
to share their stories, and all of
the stories yet to be told.*

CONTENTS

Beyond Diversity . . .

"There is always light. If only we're brave enough to see it. If only we're brave enough to be it."

— *AMANDA GORMAN, AMERICAN POET*

AUTHORS' NOTE

This ambitious book exists because more than two hundred people were willing to engage in difficult conversations. In January of 2021, we all gathered at the first annual Non-Obvious Beyond Diversity Summit. The ideas in this book are inspired by the themes we explored across that week-long virtual event.

Race, identity, gender, discrimination, equity, belonging and love are deeply emotional topics. To discuss them candidly in the company of others requires bravery.

Yet we know that creating a more equitable society has to go *beyond* conversation. Together with an amazing team of contributors, we wrote this book to imagine solutions and inspire actions. An inclusive world is worth making. Let's get started building it together.

— **Rohit and Jennifer**

FEATURED VOICES ▬▬▬▬

Michael Akinyele · Debra Alfarone · Samina Ali · Zaheer Ali · Jesse Cameron Alick · Rajesh Anandan · Luis Arandia · Seth Arndorfer · Chhavi Arya · Leonor Ayala Polley · Andrius Alvarez-Backus · Jacqueline Baker · Sanchita Balachandran · Pun Bandhu · Bennett D. Bennett · Rohit Bhargava · Shirley Bloomfield · Melissa Boone · Edith Bracho-Sanchez · Isabel Bradbury · Nicole Brewer · Hollie-Anne Brooks · Marisa Brown · Jennifer Brown · Mike Brown · Leigh-Ann Buchanan · Agata Buras · Cerrie Burnell · Lydia Caldana · Diana Caldarescu · Courtney Caldwell · Stacy Campbell · David Campt · Brittany Castaneda · Sacha Chadwick · Aneesh Chaganty · Ragen Chastain · Angela Chee · Maha Chehlaoui · Nathania Christy · Joseph Clift · Isha Cogborn · Carol Fishman Cohen · Marc Cohen · Rebecca Cokley · Beth Comstock · Charlene Polite Corley · Henry Coutinho-Mason · Joy Arlene Cox · Courtney Craven · Jan Mercer Dahms · Karen Dahms · Deniese Davis · Jessica DeGroot · Zora DeHorter · Caroline Dettman · Turquoise Devereaux · Kate Devlin · Jessica Doyle · Natalie Egan · Brandy Eggan · Kety Esquivel · Laura Evans Manatos · Simon Fenwick · Daniele Fiandaca · Hajj Flemings · Ayana Flewellen · Kwame Fluker · Aaron Foley · Leslie Forde · Dwana Franklin-Davis · Augie Gastelum · James Geurts · Bianca Ghose · Miranda Gohh · Indrani Goradia · Kishonna Gray · Stephen Green · Frank Gruber · Winona Guo · Alisa Gus · Yasaman Haghighat · Denise Hamilton · Julian Harcourt · Cortney Harding · Kerry Harrison · Felecia Hatcher · Rachel Higham · Quita Highsmith · Travis Holoway · Sabra Horne · Jackie Huba · Chipo Hwami · Kate Isler · Sahar Jahani · Sandhya Jain-Patel · Shelina Janmohamed · Veena Jayadeva · Emma Johnson · Seb Joseph · Vimbayi Kajese ·

Allison Kalloo • Allyson Kapin • Lindsay Kaplan • Alana Karen • Sheila Kasasa • Amy Kean • Becky Kekula • Sami Khan • Thembe Khumalo • Song Kim • Heather Krause • Pooja Kumar • Leela Ladnier • Myra LalDin • Miah Langlois • Scott Lanum • Melody Lewis • Brendan Lewis • Dorcas Lind • Janice Lintz • Tiffany Lung • MJ Lyons • Mita Mallick • Christopher Manente • Debbie Nez Manuel • Christopher E. Manuel • Claudia Marks • Chrisel Martinez • Wendy Mayhew • Pamhi Mbanga • Charlotte McClain-Nhlapo • Leila McKenzie-Delis • Shannie Mears • Parag Mehta • Michael Mejias • Meera Menon • Jacqueline Mgido • Simon Minty • Dino Myers-Lamptey • Paolo Nagari • Mamoudou N'Diaye • Matt Ney • Marlon Nichols • Catherine Nicolaou • Zahra Noorbakhsh • Sue Obeidi • Lindsay Orosz • Waylon Pahona Jr. • Maulik Pancholy • Rohi Mirza Pandya • Lydia Dean Pilcher • Joy Pope • Lylliam Posadas • Beny Poy • Ludmila Praslova • Marilyn Price • Alex Prout • Deepa Purushothaman • Suresh Raj • Ripa Rashid • Y. Shireen Razack • Neil Redding • Scarlett Richards • Jennifer Risi • Andrea Roane • Kate Roberts • Sergio Rosario • Christina Ryan • Monica Sack • Kaleena Sales • Monika Samtani • Kate Sánchez • Jyoti Sarda • Sabina Shah • Zharia Shinn • Martyn Sibley • Anupy Singla • Pamela Slim • JJ Snow • Gigi Sohn • Yennie Solheim • Sree Sreenivasan • James Stellar • Bonnie Stetz • Tracy Stuckrath • Amir Sulaiman • Yonta Taiwo • Alexander Taylor • Jordan Thierry • Tash Thomas • Juhu Thukral • India Thusi • José Velasco • AnaSofía Villanueva • Priya Vulchi • Elsa Waithe • Angela Ward • Chloé Skye Weisser • Brenda Darden Wilkerson • Arthur Woods • Tiffany Yu • Maysoon Zayid • Johanna Zeilstra

LEARN MORE ABOUT ALL THESE VOICES AT WWW.NONOBVIOUSDIVERSITY.COM/SPEAKERS

FULL LIST OF SESSIONS FROM THE 1st NON-OBVIOUS BEYOND DIVERSITY SUMMIT

STORYTELLING

❯ Sharing the Stage: #manels and More Inclusive Conference Speakers

❯ How to Own Your Creative Vision – Interview with Aneesh Chaganty

❯ Casting Calls: How to Include Underrepresented Voices in Film & TV

❯ Flipping the Script: Monika Samtani with Meera Menon + Deniese Davis

❯ Backstage: Lifting the Curtain on Theater's Diversity Problem

❯ Changing the Narrative: The Fight for More Diversity in Book Publishing

❯ Bigger Stories: Supporting More Diversity in Journalism + News Media

IDENTITY

❯ Just Be You: Embracing Our Bodies and Ourselves, Just as We Are

❯ Our Body is Power: Creating a Positive Representation of Ourselves

❯ Work It Out: Making Health and Fitness More Inclusive

❯ Shady Choices: Colorism and the Shifting "Face" of Fashion Brands

FAMILY

❯ Cultural Confidence: Teaching Youth to Be Proud of Their Heritage

❯ Ending Gender Based Violence: Interview with Indrani Goradia

❯ Anti-Dad? The Persistent Bias Against Fathers in The Workplace

❯ Shared Parenting: How the Pandemic Shifted Family Life Balance

❯ How To Talk to Racists: Interview with Dr. David Campt

LEADERSHIP

❯ Leading Diversity: How to Make Large Organizations More Inclusive

❯ Breaking Through: How to Mentor & Champion More Women at Work

❯ Lost In Translation: How to Lead a Diverse & Inclusive Team

❯ How to Lead Diverse Teams: Rohit Bhargava with Beth Comstock

❯ Supporting Female Executives – Interview with Deepa Purushothaman

CULTURE

❯ How To Create a More Inclusive World: Rohit Bhargava w/ Maysoon Zayid

❯ Rethinking the Way Muslims Are Portrayed in Media & Entertainment

❯ Now United: How a Global Pop Music Group Brings the World Together

❯ New Flavors: The Role of Food in Creating a More Inclusive World

❯ Is Diversity Funny? How Comedians of Color Navigate a Sensitive Topic

❯ Remembering The Past: How Museums Amplify Diversity Conversations

❯ How Rock Stars Build Their Ensemble: Interview with Stacy Campbell

WATCH THESE SESSIONS ONLINE!
www.nonobviousdiversity.com

EDUCATION
- ❯ Starting Early: Why Creating Diverse Content for Kids Matters
- ❯ Diversity at College: How to Make Higher Education More Inclusive
- ❯ How To Teach Racial Literacy with Priya Vulchi and Winona Guo

RETAIL
- ❯ Bringing More Diverse Perspectives into Marketing, PR and Advertising
- ❯ Diversity In Retail: Creating More Welcoming Experiences for All
- ❯ Visualizing Diversity: How the Marketing Imagery Is Changing

WORKPLACE
- ❯ Master Collaborators: Leadership Lessons from Disabled Trailblazers
- ❯ Hire Equity: Transforming the Recruiting Process to Be More Inclusive
- ❯ Unique Talent: Neurodiversity in The Modern Workplace
- ❯ Never Too Old: Ageism + Integrating Older Talent into The Workforce
- ❯ How Men Can Be Better Advocates for Gender Equality

TECHNOLOGY
- ❯ Women in Tech: How to Get More Women into the Tech Industry
- ❯ Everyone Welcome: Using Tech to Create More Inclusive Workplaces
- ❯ Technically Biased: Solving the Plague of Algorithmic Bias in Technology
- ❯ Safe Havens: What Gaming Communities Teach Us About Inclusion

ENTREPRENEURSHIP
- ❯ Getting Funded: How Investors Support Diverse Startup Founders
- ❯ Main Street 2.0: Building Equitable and Inclusive Economic Engines
- ❯ The Rural Renaissance: How Rural Communities Get Connected

GOVERNMENT
- ❯ Represented: How Politics and Government Is Becoming More Diverse
- ❯ Social Impact and Racial Justice in the Age of Diversity
- ❯ How Diversity Fuels Bright Ideas for the Federal Government
- ❯ Health Equity: Why Diversity Matters in Public Health

FUTURE
- ❯ Toward the Future Normal: Futurists Share Diversity Predictions
- ❯ Diverse City: How to Create More Inclusive Cities of the Future
- ❯ Robot Citizens: How Artificial Beings Will Challenge Our Perceptions

CONTRIBUTORS

 ROHIT BHARGAVA (he/him) is on a mission to inspire more non-obvious thinking in the world. He is the founder of the Non-Obvious Company, a popular keynote speaker, and the #1 WSJ bestselling author of seven books on marketing, trends and the how to predict the future.

 JENNIFER BROWN (she/her) and her team at Jennifer Brown Consulting are committed to building more inclusive and representative workplaces of belonging where everyone can thrive. She is a bestselling author and inspirational keynoter on leadership courage and change.

 ANDRIUS ALVAREZ-BACKUS (he/him) is a content writer, research assistant, and graphic designer at Jennifer Brown Consulting. He is currently studying fine art at The Cooper Union in New York City.

 CHHAVI ARYA (she/her) is the co-founder of Ideapress Publishing and the producer of the Non-Obvious Beyond Diversity Summit. She spent 10 years teaching elementary school, pioneering diversity curriculum and programming that was used across Ontario, Canada.

KAREN DAHMS (she/her) is a writer, researcher, advocate and change agent for social justice and diversity, equity and inclusion. She is the Senior Research Director at Jennifer Brown Consulting.

SANDHYA JAIN-PATEL (she/her) is a passionate DEI professional devoted to culturally accurate storytelling in media and entertainment. She is co-founder and managing director of SRC Partners.

KALEENA SALES (she/her) is an author, illustrator, and graphic design educator at Tennessee State University, an HBCU in Nashville, TN. Her research focuses on minority culture and aesthetics.

MONIKA SAMTANI (she/her) is the CEO of Ms. Media and co-founder of The Fem Word. As a media and entertainment professional, building a culture of authenticity is rooted in her work—producing, storytelling, publicity, coaching, and speaking.

ZHARIA SHINN (she/her) is a portrait collage artist based in NY. With a BFA from RISD, her vibrant collages defy pre-existing notions of beauty and promote inclusivity of the African Diaspora.

Our Words . . .

The language we use to describe situations, people, and issues is important. It can signal judgment and fuel division, or it can offer empathy and create dialogue.

Throughout this book we have tried to be thoughtful about our words. Every term, capitalization, or label was chosen with intention and tested not only by our team of contributors but also with nearly a dozen sensitivity readers.

To learn more about our language choices, turn to the appendix at the end of this book.

INTRODUCTION

"If there is a book that you want to read, but it hasn't been written yet, you must be the one to write it."
— TONI MORRISON

On a cavernous soundstage in Denmark, groups of people file in one by one. They are clearly different from one another. One group walks in with tattoos. Another, all female, is wearing medical uniforms in various colors. There is an all-White group, right alongside one that includes people visibly from multiple ethnicities. Each group stands apart, staring uncomfortably at one another for what seems like an eternity.

Finally, a host comes in to explain what is about to happen.

"I'm going to ask you some questions today," he says. "Some of them may be a bit personal, but I hope you will answer them honestly."

The first question immediately reduces the tension. "Which one of you was the class clown?" A smattering of people from each cluster comes forward. They line up together on the far side of the room and stand in front of a screen posing for a group photo. The session continues with a range of other unexpected questions. Who among you are stepparents? Who has been bullied? Who has *been* a bully? Who feels lonely? After each question, people come together, embrace, pose for a photograph, and return to their group.

The point of the exercise soon becomes clear to every participant: they are celebrating their similarities instead of their differences.

 Watch the TV2 social experiment video at www.nonobviousdiversity.com/resources.

This social experiment was conceived and filmed several years ago to promote Denmark's most-watched family of channels, TV2. Titled "All That We Share," the campaign ran on Danish television and was later released globally on YouTube.[1] It quickly went viral, racking up nearly 300 million views and winning a prestigious Gold Cannes Lion award.

This focus on similarities is sadly missing in many conversations happening about diversity and inclusion across the world. It is a rarely spotlighted irony that so much of the dialogue about diversity ends up emphasizing what sets us apart instead.

You can see this splintered approach in the structure of many live and virtual events aimed at exploring the theme of diversity. There are conferences dedicated to racial justice, reducing gender discrimination at work, advocating for LGBTQ+ legislation, eliminating ageism at work, creating more accessible digital content for people with disabilities, making corporate boards more inclusive, and much more.

These conferences host important conversations—and they offer a safe space for people who have been excluded and marginalized to share their experiences freely and have their points of view heard and discussed. They play an essential role in our evolving conversation about diversity and equity.

And yet, they are not enough.

These often-insular conversations about diversity don't reflect the reality of our intersecting identities. As the TV2 viral experiment so powerfully illustrates, none of us fits neatly into a single category. We exist through intersections, but our conversations about diversity regularly push us to pick one dimension of ourselves at the expense of others. These dimensions are the lenses that shape how we perceive our place in the world. Being Hispanic, or female, or gay, or over 50, or disabled, or any combination of identities helps us zoom in on a unique perspective of the world. But while zoom lenses are helpful for focusing on details, they are intentionally designed to ignore the full picture.

If there is one shortcoming of the worldwide conversation about diversity and inclusion, it is this: focusing on only one aspect of our identities prevents the opportunity to better understand ourselves and others outside that one label.

Instead, there is a concept we will discuss frequently in this book known as *intersectionality*. The term, first coined by American lawyer and civil rights advocate Kimberlé Williams Crenshaw, refers to the idea that none of us can be defined by a single label, but only through a combination of social identities.

Embracing the idea of intersectionality requires us to switch to a wide-angle lens. What if we had conferences, TV shows, or corporate recruiting programs dedicated to bringing people and perspectives together that might never otherwise share the same space? It is exciting to imagine the sorts of questions and topics that might arise.

How would someone fighting to end gender pay gaps relate to a disabled gamer demanding more accessible experiences? What would an advocate for racial literacy in schools say to a researcher studying how to end age-related biases at work? What might a local business fighting to expand broadband internet access for those living on Native American reservations ask a community organizer imagining how to transform a neglected local park into a vibrant urban garden? All of these people are pioneers fighting for equity, but they rarely (if ever) cross paths.

To truly create a more inclusive world, we need to move beyond the usual diversity conversations and break down the barriers between these topics.

"Sometimes the assumptions we make about others come not from what we have been told or what we have seen on television or in books, but rather from what we have not been told."

Dr. Beverly Daniel Tatum, Author and Psychologist

Vernā Myers, vice president of inclusion strategy at Netflix, once said, "diversity is being invited to the party; inclusion is being asked to dance." Her words are often shared by those who advocate for diversity, but for us, they inspired a question: what if everyone was not only invited to the party and asked to dance, but also left with a mixtape filled with music they would love, but had never had the chance to hear before?

In late 2020, we decided to try and host this type of party. It started with the idea of a one-day virtual event that would bring together a dozen or so diversity and inclusion experts from various fields. Over the next few months, that concept sparked a whirlwind of hundreds of conversations and 20-hour-days that would eventually result in the groundbreaking gathering of voices that inspired this book. It all began, as many great ideas do, with listening.

The World's Most Ambitious Conversation About Diversity

In 2020, an app called Clubhouse started to take off. A real-time audio chat room where anyone can start a conversation, the app owed much of its rapid growth to early popularity with Black creators and musicians. As a result, users of Clubhouse were highly likely to enter "rooms" on the platform and hear conversations hosted by people whose diverse opinions and expertise were frequently missing from mainstream media.

Plunging into this never-ending stream of conversations, at any given moment you could hear struggling professionals grappling with bias in the workplace, while minutes later, you might join a group of parents talking about accepting their transgender kids. In a single afternoon, you could participate in conversations about neurodivergent education, hear immigration questions from refugees, experience the daily heroism of doctors working on the front lines to fight COVID-19, debate cultural appropriation and learn about income inequality.

These are topics many of us who have contributed to this book deal with every day in our work. To add even more authentic perspectives to our efforts, we augmented our daily conversations about diversity, equity and inclusion (DEI) by dipping in and out of rooms on Clubhouse and listening to real people share their experiences and challenges. We also spent the past year participating in virtual conferences, professional webinars, and training sessions centered on DEI. We read dozens of reports, books and magazine articles.

Finally we started putting together a list of topics for our virtual event. It grew quickly: Women in tech. Inclusive higher education. Colorism in fashion. Body shaming. Neurodiverse recruiting. Accessible gaming. Workplace ageism. Racial justice. Image bias. Pay equity. Gender fluidity. White fragility. Social belonging. Diverse casting. Representative government. The list goes on.

Along the way, we discovered meaningful conversations already happening about all these topics amongst experts and advocates. We discovered that most of them were happening in isolation, completely separate from one another. It was like seeing an entire relay contest of athletes racing side by side, with no one passing any batons. It became clear that creating a conversation where we connected the dots between these topics would necessitate something more significant than gathering a dozen smart people together for one day. So we sent out more inquiries to more people and engaged the help of additional experts to expand our vision.

By the time the virtual event was broadcast live in late January 2021, we had lined up just over 200 speakers who participated in more than 50 sessions. Over 75 percent described themselves as belonging to an underrepresented group. More than two-thirds identified as a gender other than male. The range of expertise and topics represented was equally diverse.

Our panel of experts included a widely loved news anchor, a world record holder as the heaviest person to complete a marathon, multiple chief diversity officers, the popular voice of an animated children's TV show character, a master puppeteer, a child abuse survivor, a former Miss India winner and two hundred others.

 Watch all 50+ sessions from the summit at www.nonobviousdiversity.com/resources

We called the event the "Non-Obvious Beyond Diversity Summit." It was *Non-Obvious* because of the types of conversations we hoped to curate. And it went *Beyond Diversity*, because we knew that if we were truly going to have an impact, we needed to focus every conversation on tangible actions we could all take to build a more inclusive world. Our tagline came from one of our speakers who remarked that the event sounded like "the world's most ambitious conversation about diversity."

Our "ambitious" conversation was a hit.

Thousands of people watched the event live and commented on the sessions in real time, and hundreds of thousands watched them on demand in the months afterward. But the day after the summit ended, we knew our work had only begun. To share the insights we heard with a wider audience, we started working on this book. The first step was to identify twelve themes that cut across all the sessions. Then we assembled a team of expert contributors and started writing.

The book you hold in your hands is the final product. It is a compilation of conversations that we hope will launch you into a journey to understand people unlike yourself. For us, and perhaps for you as well, it usually starts with a moment of awakening.

Where Every Diversity Journey Starts . . .

You may be thinking that the path to experiencing this moment is someone else's journey to take. Maybe you come from a marginalized group yourself. Some of you might even be DEI experts. Or you may already consider yourself to be an ally and advocate for equity and inclusion through your actions or beliefs. Wherever you are on your journey, we hope this book and the stories in it will inspire and motivate you to learn more, speak up and take action.

"The ultimate tragedy is not the oppression and cruelty by the bad people, but the silence over that by the good people."

■■■■■■ Martin Luther King, Jr., Social Activist and Nobel Prize Winner

The first thing you should know is that this book was compiled, edited and reviewed by dozens of people who believe in the power of standing up for others. The voices you will see spotlighted in this book regularly spend their days helping others to be more open-minded, inclusive and empathetic toward those from different backgrounds. We all live and breathe this work . . . and yet for each of us, the process of writing this book has offered a moment of awakening that we very much needed.

No human is free from bias. What we all must try to do is recognize and overcome our biases and to see others as having equal potential.

In the fight for equity, there have always been three parties. Two are well understood. There are the *oppressors,* who benefit from inequity and leverage their power to maintain the status quo. And there are the *oppressed* who fight back—sometimes successfully and sometimes not. These two have been the participants in every social movement everywhere in the world, whether against racism and gender-based discrimination or ethnic struggles between majorities and minorities.

Yet there is, and has always been, a third regularly overlooked group: the *bystanders.* These are the people and institutions who remain on the sidelines by choice or ignorance. Many tell themselves that the fight isn't their fight. They may not be racist, but they are also not anti-racist. These are the bystanders, and their willful silence has also contributed to and shaped human history. It is time for that to change.

This is a book about being more than a bystander.

No matter what combination of ethnic, social, gender or cultural groups you belong to, this book aims to help you and the people around you achieve a moment of awakening. Perhaps it may help to start by sharing some of our own.

For Rohit, one of these moments came when he became embroiled in controversy just months before our summit. In 2020, he accepted an invitation to deliver a recorded virtual keynote at an event in Asia about the future of marketing. When the organizers shared an image on social media promoting the entire list of headlining speakers, it was obvious that every one of them was male. The social media backlash started instantly.

Some commenters called for a boycott of the entire event. Others noted the irony of having only male speakers at an event for an industry that, by most estimates, is more than 50 percent female. Dozens suggested that the speakers themselves be held personally responsible for their complicity in agreeing to speak on a #manel (a male-only panel).

Despite years of work supporting and writing about more inclusivity in business, Rohit hadn't thought to check if women were represented on stage at a conference he had agreed to speak at. He didn't realize his mistake—until someone else pointed it out. Rohit apologized and immediately helped the event organizers seek out female speakers to include. He also converted his solo session into a panel discussion by inviting two female trend researchers from his network to share the stage as co-presenters.

The moment reminded Rohit that no matter what work he may have done in the past, being a vocal ally is a constant challenge. Today, he is a popular keynote speaker and the founder of the Non-Obvious Company where he leads a team that produces content, workshops and signature events designed to help leaders embrace "non-obvious" perspectives and see what others miss.

"If you have come here to help me, you are wasting your time. But if you have come because your liberation is bound up with mine, then let us work together."

Lilla Watson, Murri (Indigenous Australian) Artist and Activist

Jennifer recalls a similar moment of awakening to the reality that the identities we carry can marginalize and separate us from the mainstream. When she came out as a member of the LGBTQ+ community in her 20s, Jennifer downplayed this part of her identity in a series of professional roles, from opera singer to corporate HR professional to entrepreneur. She saw few people who shared her story—at least publicly—and she didn't feel safe bringing her full identity to the workplace.

Discovering the LGBTQ+ workplace equality movement shaped the way she understood her own story of not feeling heard or respected. The sad reality is that today's work culture remains ill-suited to people from marginalized communities.

When Jennifer founded her own consulting company 15 years ago, her struggle for authenticity continued in what was a largely male-dominated space. She initially built a traditional hierarchy with many of her mentors and key hires being White men. She felt vulnerable about her identity as a new entrepreneur and a queer woman, and feared prospective clients would hold stereotypes or biases that might hamper her credibility or impact.

At the same time she came to recognize the privilege and advantages she holds as a White cisgender woman. She understood that privilege isn't just about what you've experienced personally during your lifetime; it's also about what you haven't had to experience.

Today Jennifer describes herself as an "aspiring ally," and taking action against discrimination and inequities has become the mission of her company. Jennifer Brown Consulting is a highly diverse company—led by a diverse team—and has become a recognized leader in diversity, equity, and inclusion, working with hundreds of companies. Jennifer has become a renowned speaker, has written several books on diversity and inclusion, and she continually uses her platform to amplify the voices of underrepresented communities.

We are each many identities at once, and each one can influence our actions. At the same time, we all carry some degree of privilege. In moments when that privilege is laid bare, we can choose to silently benefit and remain a bystander, or we can stand up and try to fix something that is clearly wrong.

"To never think about race means that it doesn't really shape your life, or more specifically, the race you have is not a burden to you."

▬▬▬▬▬▬ Kimberlé Williams Crenshaw, Professor, Advocate and Author

The ambition of this book is to inspire you to take action when that moment comes for you—or even better, to create that moment for yourself.

How To Read This Book . . .

In the chapters that follow, you'll read about twelve themes that are shaping our world today. For each topic, we will explore how it is, how it could be, what needs to change on a systemic level (imperatives), and what you can do today to help bring about this change (actions).

This is not a research book. This is a do-something book.

By spotlighting the conversations that are already taking place and celebrating those who are making strides in the world of diversity, equity and inclusion, we hope to amplify their work, provide concrete and actionable strategies, and give you a roadmap to becoming personally involved.

By ending each chapter with specific "Conversation Starters," we are hoping to spark new conversations that offer opportunities to align these important but isolated efforts.

The journey to build a more inclusive world must involve all of us. Along the way we will need to better understand culture, identity and family. We will have to ask big questions about how technology, government, education and our workplaces are structured. Entrepreneurship, leadership and the retail landscape that surround us also must be part of this conversation. And it all starts, in our humble opinion, by reimagining the stories we tell and share with the world.

Our lives, ultimately, are lived through our stories. So let's get started in crafting a better and more inclusive one together.

BEYOND DIVERSITY IN
STORYTELLING

"'Diversity' should just be called 'reality.' Your books, your TV shows, your movies, your articles, your curricula, need to reflect reality."

**— Tananarive Due,
Author and American Book Award winner**

Chapter Summary:

Representation in storytelling matters. The characters portrayed in fiction and the way cultures are covered in news media shape our perceptions of everything. An inclusive world must therefore start by reinventing the stories we choose to tell, consume and share.

How It Is . . .

In the final days of December each year, thousands of competitors gather in Saudi Arabia for the King Abdulaziz Falconry Festival. Known as the "sport of kings," the ancient art of falconry uses trained raptors to hunt and return prey to captivity. It is a millennia-old sport practiced by cultures across the globe . . . and usually by men.

But in 2020, there was one participant among the many falconers at the event who made international headlines—Athari Alkhaldi, the first woman to ever qualify.[1]

Alkhaldi herself recognized the significance of her entry: "With my participation . . . I proved I am here, that women can join this field, that it's not only restricted to men," she shared with global media while standing with her falcon, Ma'aned.

At approximately the same time, a British jockey named Rachael Blackmore broke another barrier by becoming the first woman to win the challenging Grand National horse race in England.[2] These types of barrier-breaking stories, once a rarity, now seem to be shared regularly.

A scan of worldwide media on any given day offers plenty of examples. A hip-hop musical from Puerto Rican musician Lin-Manuel Miranda passes $1B in revenue. African American poet Amanda Gorman is selected to speak at the 2020 US Presidential inauguration. Fifteen-year-old Swedish climate activist Greta

Thunberg rises to international prominence, while referring to her diagnosis of Asperger syndrome as her "superpower."

Taken together, these inspiring examples illustrate how storytelling can be the most potent way to celebrate progress, inspire change, and bring about a more diverse world.

They also raise an important question: what about the thousands of stories like these that remain untold? If stories shape our perceptions, then perhaps the stories we never hear shape our biases through the lack of awareness they perpetuate.

"Storytelling forces readers to come in and experience this entirely new world . . . it's a place where we connect with one another on a human level."

Samina Ali, Author, Curator, and Speaker

Beyond the stories we read, our worldviews commonly come from the movies we watch, the news we follow, or the events we attend (either virtually or in-person). We constantly surround ourselves with an ever-growing collection of stories. When told skillfully, they can offer us a sense of connection with others and a feeling of acceptance for ourselves.

All too often, however, the stories we hear aren't being told by the people who have truly lived them. As a result, those same lived experiences can be marginalized or depicted in unrealistic ways.

When people's stories are told from the perspective of an outsider, they can reinforce negative stereotypes.

In early 2020, we saw an example of this in the literary world: backlash brewed when a novel about a Mexican migrant journey called *American Dirt* was selected for Oprah's Book Club.

It started with writer and podcaster Myriam Gurba calling out the book's White author for her self-described ambition of giving voice to the "faceless brown mass" of migrants at the Mexican border.

Writing critically about the novel's main character, Lydia, Gurba pointed out that she "experiences shock after shock when confronted with the realities of México, realities that would not shock a Mexican . . . she perceives her own country through the eyes of a pearl-clutching American tourist."[3]

"As a Latina writer, I'm very often asked to make my stories more relevant . . . when the publishing industry is 80 percent White, what I'm really being asked to do is to make my stories more relevant to White people."[4]

Julissa Arce, Author and Co-Founder of Ascend Educational Fund

The portrayal of non-White, one-dimensional characters like Lydia by White storytellers is not uncommon, and the implications of these portrayals are serious for the groups they are intended to represent. The history of film is filled with similar examples.

Native Americans have been typecast as barbaric warriors or enemies in Westerns. Men with Eastern European accents frequently play villains. Our stories cannot become more diverse and inclusive if the characters inside them are reduced to stereotypes.

When these biased portrayals carry over from fictional realities into lived ones through biased representation in the news media, the ramifications for real people can be life or death.

Nielsen, a media metrics company that studies ratings and television audiences, conducted a study in March of 2021 titled "What You See Isn't What You Get: The Role of Media in Anti-Asian Racism."[5] The study suggests that the number of times we see minorities on screen, and the context of their roles, contributes to harmful beliefs that can lead to bias in real life.

Only 18.8% of all print and digital newsroom managers are people of color.

Source: 2019 ASNE Newsroom Diversity Survey

When vulnerable groups are scapegoated by the news media, it becomes dangerously easy to blame those groups for society's problems.

The problem stems from who is reporting the news. When newsroom editors and writers lack varied perspectives, it impacts the way news is covered and reported. News stories can be incomplete or compromised by their gaps in understanding.

Or worse, they can actively promote harmful stereotypes about entire communities of people.

The impact of inadequate representation in news reporting can also result in biased headlines and coverage until they are exposed by someone with a more balanced perspective.

A perfect example can be seen in the tweets of Patrick Gathara—a Kenyan journalist who cleverly uses Twitter to rewrite the headlines for American news stories with the same inherently biased and judgmental language that Western media has used for years when reporting on Africa. Here are two examples:

gathara ✅
@gathara
· · ·

Replying to @gathara

#BREAKING Local reporter says youth militia roaming streets of beleaguered US capital, Washington DC, and terrorising residents, are worrying reminders of the deeply divided, politically unstable, debt-ridden country's potential for savage ethnic violence.

gathara ✅
@gathara
· · ·

Replying to @gathara

#BREAKING Canada extends the closure of its border with the US and puts its security forces on high alert in anticipation of a new wave of American refugees as ethnic violence flares up once again in its volatile, covid-ravaged, neighbour where 300,000 people have already died.

The impact of bias in the stories we listen to is the same, whether it happens in the headlines of global newspapers or the filmed scenes of Hollywood blockbusters. In both cases, underrepresented voices do not see their stories reflected, and even when they *are* portrayed, they see themselves shown in a deeply problematic light.

"Representation in the fictional world signifies social existence; absence means symbolic annihilation."

George Gerbner, Professor and Founder of Cultivation Theory

To explore these issues, our summit brought together experts from a variety of fields, including journalism, publishing, film & television, and literary publishing. Their insights fueled our conclusion that it is stories above all else that offer us the best starting point to shape a more inclusive world.

How Things Are Changing . . .

From the screen and stage to the books we read, story creators are beginning to prioritize authentic diversity.

To demonstrate both the issue at hand and how our responses to it are changing, consider the example of Apu Nahasapeemapetilon from the long-running American TV show *The Simpsons*.

Apu's character is that of an Indian immigrant who runs a convenience store, and his exaggerated accent has been voiced for decades by White actor Hank Azaria. The character's depiction on the show has been widely critiqued as a racist, harmful stereotype by the Indian American and greater Desi community. The issue was even highlighted in the 2017 documentary *The Problem with Apu*, written by and starring South Asian comedian Hari Kondabolu.

In 2020, Azaria responded to the public pressure generated by this documentary and other critiques, by announcing he would no longer voice the character of Apu. Alongside his announcement, the creators of *The Simpsons* pledged that they would no longer hire White actors to voice non-White characters.[6]

66% of speaking roles in major Hollywood films in 2019 went to White characters.

Source: 2019 USC Annenberg Inclusion Initiative

This is not an isolated example. The entire casting process in Hollywood is undergoing significant changes both in how roles are cast and the opportunities afforded to talent from underrepresented backgrounds. Their right to audition and be considered for all types of roles, not merely those that minimize them into sidekicks or typecast them as villains, is being given greater attention.

The psychological thriller *Run* featured a disabled lead character played by disabled actress Kiera Allen. According to director and writer Aneesh Chaganty, casting a disabled actress in the lead role had a huge impact on the authenticity with which her character's story was told and shaped much of the filming process.

"Disabled people are still usually played by nondisabled people, and most of those roles are of White disabled people . . . society must take responsibility to work with us, and ensure that the media more accurately represents us."

Judy Heumann, Disability Justice Leader and Author

According to BoxOfficeGuru.com Editor Gitesh Pandya, the top-grossing box office hit when US theaters started to reopen after the height of the pandemic was *Godzilla vs Kong*. The film's popularity was driven by a racially diverse audience, with polling on the day of release showing more than 66 percent of the audience to be people of color.

According to a study by the Annenberg Inclusion Initiative, Disney's female-centered films and those featuring underrepresented lead characters were box office frontrunners,[7] with more than $6 billion earned globally.

A similar hunger for diversely told stories is shaping the news media audience, as well. Blavity is one example of an emerging digital news platform focused on communities of color and covering issues ranging from news, politics, and social justice to travel, lifestyle, technology, and film. In May of 2020, as the Black Lives Matter Movement resurged and other outlets were struggling to report meaningful stories, Blavity brought in 38 million pageviews, up 150 percent from the previous month.[8]

NBC Universal is also investing in supporting this shift across the news media industry with their 2021 announcement of NBCU Academy—a multi-year partnership to provide journalism training and development to 17 academic partners including Historically Black Colleges and Universities (HBCUs), Hispanic-Serving Institutions and colleges with significant Latino, Asian American and Pacific Islander, Black, Indigenous and tribal populations. As NBC Newsgroup Executive Editor Leonor Ayala Polley shared at our summit, "we put our subject matter experts front and center to teach, to mentor, to help those aspiring journalists go from the classroom to the newsroom."

The trajectory is clear. Stories which have been buried for so long (and those who tell them) are finding new homes, audiences, and fans, both inside and outside of the demographic groups they represent.

What Needs To Happen . . .

In 2021, Netflix commissioned a study with USC Annenberg Inclusion Initiative founder Dr. Stacy L. Smith on inclusion behind and in front of the lens. As a result of her findings, the streaming giant committed $100M to help "set up underrepresented communities for success in TV and film industries" over the next five years.[9]

Commitments like this open the door a little further for more diverse storytellers to share their work.

"Representation matters, on screen or on stage. We are seeing empowerment of underrepresented communities across Hollywood and audiences are demanding more inclusive storytelling."

Rohi Mirza Pandya, Producer and Co-Founder, SRC Partners

So what needs to happen to keep this momentum going? Here are a few ideas.

IMPERATIVE #1

Systemic financial barriers that exclude diverse storytellers must be exposed and removed.

While the push for greater equity in all forms of storytelling is far from new, it has been gaining traction over the past few years. For example, in 2019, writers across the country began using the hashtag #PublishingPaidMe to share their book advances on social media and expose racial pay disparities in the publishing industry.[10]

Some White authors disclosed that they'd been paid hundreds of thousands of dollars for their debut books, whereas acclaimed authors of color shared that they'd had to fight to get even a fraction of the same pay for their second or third publications.

The posts soon grew into an industry-wide conversation around financial investment in authors of color.

In a similar example of collective dialogue, the hashtag #OscarsSoWhite went viral in 2015 as a criticism of the glaring lack of diversity in nominations for the Academy Awards that year. The tag sparked a hot debate over whose stories are welcomed in Hollywood (and by extension, American society as a whole) and which stories are left out.[11]

The #PublishingPaidMe conversation was started by L.L. McKinney, a Black author specializing in young adult literature; #OscarsSoWhite was launched by April Reign, a Black media strategist and DEI advocate. Neither McKinney nor Reign were major power brokers in their industries, yet their efforts to hold entire institutions accountable garnered global attention and galvanized hundreds of thousands of people to contribute their own stories to the conversation. The message from their fight to expose inequity is clear.

76% of publishing professionals in America are White, 81% are straight, and 89% are non-disabled.

Source: Leeandlow 2019

If you see certain stories being excluded or unfairly compensated, use your voice to call out the injustice.

Raising awareness of inequity on a systemic level always starts with the determination of individuals to make the problem known.

Entrenched biases in media must be *consciously* acknowledged and addressed.

As humans, we all have subjective, ingrained beliefs that inform our decision-making, even if we aren't aware of them. The problem is that the one-sided media we consume can end up confirming our perspectives rather than challenging them.[12]

The growing reliance on social media as a news source makes this problem worse. Algorithms quickly calculate which perspectives you prefer, and then feed you stories that reinforce what you already believe. More diverse perspectives may be out there, but online personalization of news feeds through algorithms makes it highly unlikely you'll ever see them.

The best way to address this type of bias is by exposing it in real time. One tangible way this is already happening is through the fact-checking tools recently added by several social media platforms to limit the spread of fake and misleading stories. Aside from automated solutions, there are also a number of organizations doing important work to spotlight biases in the media and entertainment we consume, and to solve them.

In the performing arts, institutions like the Asian American Performers Action Coalition or the African American Artists Alliance are fighting to diversify the reality of who gets to be on the stage or screen telling stories.

"I was reading tons of scripts every day and just thinking to myself, where are the brown people? Where are other people? Why aren't there Muslim women?"

Sahar Jahani, Screenwriter, Ramy, 13 Reasons Why, and The Bold Type

For the past 20+ years, BlackFacts.com has gathered tens of thousands of news articles and stories about Black history and aims to "change the way people find and explore Black history, Black culture, and soon, Black products and services." The efforts of ambitious community-led initiatives like this website or coalition groups play an important part in helping to expose entrenched biases in all forms of media.

IMPERATIVE #3

Talent pipelines need to be restructured with equity as a priority.

If people from marginalized groups are unable to advance in a homogeneous industry, organizations need to incentivize leaders to create pathways that make their industry more diverse and inclusive.

This might entail paid internships or externships, high profile mentorships and sponsorships, wage increases for underpaid team members, and/or professional development opportunities targeted to underrepresented talent to help them advance.

Proponents of inclusion often argue that simple diversity quotas won't get the job done. As Nielsen VP of Diverse Insights Charlene Polite Corley shared during our summit, "presence alone is not representation . . . it's also about the quality and context that diverse identity groups appear in the content that we view. This nuance is hard to achieve without the influence of representative talent empowered both in front of the camera, and behind the scenes."

The work of Inkluded Academy is another example of how this can be accomplished. Inkluded is a nonprofit committed to recruiting, training, placing, and retaining BIPOC (Black, Indigenous, and People of Color) talent in the publishing industry.

ColorCreative, a diversity-focused talent agency founded by producer Deniese Davis and writer Issa Rae, is another example. Their aim is to create a direct-to-industry pipeline for underrepresented writers in film and television.

"In order to tell the most authentic stories, you have to give a little bit of leeway to the creators, and the artists, and the people of color who know those stories best."

Deniese Davis, Co-Founder of ColorCreative

Each of these organizations provides a pathway to bring more diverse talent into industries that might otherwise be inaccessible.

What You Can Do...

The stories we choose to consume—and believe—shift our worldviews. Our support can have a material impact on which stories get told in the future and which storytellers get funded to share their gifts.

With that in mind, we've outlined three actionable steps that you can take either as a storyteller yourself or as a consumer of stories produced by others.

ACTION #1

Seek out more unfamiliar stories and expand your media diet.

We live in a time of target audiences, where every story seems told for a predetermined audience. When stories are dismissed as only for some people, they fail to realize their true potential. Instead of accepting these artificial barriers, we all must make a choice to actively seek out stories told from perspectives other than our own.

One specific tactic Rohit has long suggested is buying and reading magazines not meant for you. Two of his favorites— *Teen Vogue* and *Modern Farmer*—both illustrate the point.

As a non-rural father of two boys who is well beyond his teenage years, he is not the target audience for either publication. Nonetheless, reading them offers him perspectives he might not encounter otherwise.

It's extremely easy to become stuck in a storytelling rut. We read stories we agree with. We watch films with characters we identify with. Social media algorithms serve up stories that reinforce our beliefs or fuel our existing sense of outrage. The only way to break out of the cycle is to stop letting algorithms dictate the stories you allow into your life.

"It is not just about making space for diverse stories in our media diets, we must transform the way that we discover, share and celebrate those stories as well."

Maha Chehlaoui, Founder of Pass the Mic Media

What would happen if you chose to consume just one unfamiliar story every month by going to a theater show, or watching a new movie or TV show, or reading an article from a unique news source, or picking up a book about a different topic? There are many ways to expand your media diet . . . you just need to make a decision to do it.

Be more intentional about the stories you share and consume.

Beyond shifting what stories you choose to consume, it is also important for you to consider what stories you are promoting to others.

59% of links shared on social media have never actually been clicked.

Source: Columbia University and the French National Institute

What we choose to share, particularly on social media, can become a thoughtless reflex. Instead of quickly reposting an article based on its headline, stop for a moment and consider the bigger picture of what you are sharing. Research shows the majority of social media users share stories they have never read.

Being intentional with the media we spend time watching, reading or listening to—and later recommending—is a personal choice that has more impact than we realize. Each of us possesses the power to amplify stories that might otherwise remain unheard, or to share content that reinforces stereotypes. We are all better than that. We must be.

Share your non-obvious story
with the world, when you are ready.

We all have a story to tell. This book is filled with examples of people who have bravely overcome personal reluctance, societal barriers, institutionalized discrimination or biased legislation to publicly share their own narratives.

Storytelling can be a struggle. At the same time, it can offer moments of redemption and profound self-awakening . . . not only for those consuming the stories, but also for those who speak up and tell them.

Perhaps you have a story of your own that you've kept hidden out of fear or shame. Maybe it hasn't felt like the right time, or it was simply too difficult to share. One of the biggest ambitions for this book is to offer a reminder that every individual story holds the power to change the world and inspire other people. Your story could do the same when you are ready to share it.

Our stories come in time. When you do choose to share *your* story, there will be people who are waiting to hear it—including all of us who gathered to write this book and share it with you.

Beyond Diversity In
STORYTELLING

🏛 WHAT NEEDS TO HAPPEN:

- Systemic financial barriers that exclude diverse storytellers must be exposed and removed.
- Entrenched biases in media must be consciously acknowledged and addressed.
- Talent pipelines need to be restructured with equity as a priority.

WHAT *YOU* CAN DO:

- Seek out more unfamiliar stories and expand your media diet.
- Be more intentional about the stories you share and consume.
- Share your non-obvious story with the world, when you are ready.

💬 CONVERSATION STARTERS:

- Who is one under-appreciated storyteller that you know from your cultural background but whom others might be unfamiliar with? How could you promote them?
- Find two stories from recent news about the same subject that have opposing perspectives. Why are they different, and what biases do they show?

BEYOND DIVERSITY IN
IDENTITY

"My potential is more than can be expressed within the bounds of my race or ethnic identity."
— *Arthur Ashe, American Tennis Player*

Chapter Summary:

Our identities are a spectrum that cannot be reduced to labels. Today global media increasingly encourages us to be ourselves, and the industries that once profited from manipulating our self-esteem are starting to sell authenticity instead. As a result, more people are finding safe spaces both in their personal lives and at work to embrace every part of their identity, and respecting the diverse identities of others as well.

How It Is . . .

In 2018, Bryan Elliott was recording a live interview with marketing guru Seth Godin for an episode of his popular online show, *Behind the Brand*. An experienced interviewer, Elliott had hosted hundreds of live conversations with well-known people including media mogul Arianna Huffington, legendary skateboarder Tony Hawk, and NFL quarterback Russell Wilson—but on this day, he was unusually nervous.

At the end of the interview, he decided to reveal a personal story that he had never shared before. It was a simple piece of advice that Godin gave him 10 years prior about the hard truth that "no one is coming to save you—you need to save yourself." Bryan never forgot the lesson, and it changed the trajectory of his life and helped him find a sense of true belonging. On stage, he began with a confession: "I am adopted. My entire life I always had this desire to find my birth parents. I wanted to know who I was . . . my roots, and where I come from."[1]

He went on to share his vulnerable journey of finding his birth mother, and how things didn't go as planned . . . but also of how he eventually found a new kind of peace and accepted every part of himself.

 Watch the full video of Bryan's story at www.nonobviousdiversity.com/resources.

The paths we take while discovering our identities typically start with labels. In Bryan's case, his label was *adopted*—and his experience of self-discovery centered on exploring what this one word meant to him. All of us start our lives with these types of labels that are assigned to us by others, or by the culture we live in, based on aspects of our identity.

Identity is race, gender, abilities, and sexuality. It is ethnicity and religion, marital status and political affiliation. Identity is how we wear our hair and the accents with which we speak. It is where our parents came from, how we view the world, the work we do, and the spaces we seek to occupy.

The labels assigned to us based on our identities come in many forms. Teenager. Gay. Athletic. Hispanic. Grandparent. Blind. Lawyer. Creative. Leader. Adopted.

While none of these particular labels is inherently biased or racist, sometimes they can *feel* that way when they're used in a certain context. Calling someone adopted could be a statement of fact, or it could be used to suggest they don't fit in. And there certainly *are* inherently biased or racist labels too, that can have a real and tragic impact on people's lives when they are used to demonize or exclude them.

> "Some people oppose diversity because they are bigots. Others, though, are skeptical of diversity because of how we, its champions, practice it. We're fixated on labeling. And labeling drains diversity of its unifying potential."
>
> **Irshad Manji, Author of Don't Label Me**

As we've explored the complex topic of identity in this book, we have remained intensely conscious of the power labels hold. Whenever possible, we have tried to offer a reminder that anytime labels are used, they should only be read as a starting point from which to describe a person's identity.

Labels are never the full story.

Instead of labels, psychologist Dan McAdams describes the story of our lives as our "narrative identity" and has spent decades studying how we use our own narratives to present ourselves to the world. They shape our perception of ourselves, give the world a way to describe us, and sometimes a reason to mistreat us as well.

> "Having an identity can give you a sense of how you fit into the social world. Not only does your identity give you reasons to do things, it can give others reasons to do things to you."
>
> **Kwame Anthony Appiah, Author of The Lies That Bind**

Monika Samtani, one of the contributors to this book, understands all too well the experience of being judged for her identity. At just 11 years old, she recalls her difficult first days of middle school as the first-born daughter of immigrants from India in the 1960s.

She grew up in a time when the color of her skin made her a target for the worst kind of bullying. For months she sat at lunch alone, rode to school in silence and felt isolated in a bubble of invisibility that others had decided to impose on her.

Studies have shown that the experience of having one's identity questioned or attacked, whether through sexism, racism, or other forms of discrimination, activates the same regions of the brain that respond to life-or-death survival situations. In other words, having your identity threatened literally feels like your life is in danger.

For Monika, that childhood experience propelled her future success. She would go on to spend more than two decades as a broadcast news anchor, and is currently the co-founder of an influential identity-based platform and podcast called *The Fem Word*. On her show, she currently gives other women a voice to share their identities with the world and works to make sure that no woman of any background has her identity silenced.

42% of LGBTQ youth seriously considered attempting suicide in the past twelve months.

Source: The Trevor Project National Survey on LGBTQ Youth Mental Health 2021

Lydia X.Z. Brown are also familiar with the idea of being judged through the identities assigned to them. As a writer, artist, educator, and lawyer, they are deeply involved with a variety of advocacy groups.

"As somebody who is nonbinary and trans, queer, asexual, East Asian, transracially and internationally adopted and multiply-disabled, I often find myself as the only one in communities of color who may be the only openly trans or disabled person . . . it gives me a responsibility to be accountable to the communities I come from."[2]

The pressure to show ourselves not only as we wish to be but as manifestations of the labels that people may assign to us is also the driving force behind multiple billion-dollar industries—from fashion to fitness. Self-discovery books, anti-aging creams, and auto-retouching photo apps all offer a pathway from the identity you have to the one that you want. Unfortunately, they are usually accompanied by aggressive marketing designed to make us feel inadequate. This has a predictably toxic effect on people's self-esteem.

Beauty advertising makes people feel worse about themselves to promote products that "fix" how they look. Hair-care products underscore the perception that there is something wrong with non-straightened hair. Skin-care brands sell creams to lighten skin tones, reinforcing the idea that darker skin is less desirable. Each of these industries sends the message that some identities are "better" than others.

Yet because of how noticeably biased these industries have been and how relentlessly they have manipulated our self-worth, the cultural backlash against them has been loud and is gaining momentum. As a result, all of these industries are being forced to reevaluate their *own* values, and the speed and significance of the disruption has been stunning.

How Things Are Changing . . .

The business of identity has started to intersect with the desire for authenticity. Companies that once focused on selling products and services by making us feel like *less* have now started to profit by making us feel like we can *belong*, exactly as we are.

"Fashion is a statement to the world. You are saying, this is who I am. This is what I'm about. Before they really know you, your fashion describes your identity."

Sabina Shah, Actress

Fashion brands are a prime example of this. Today it is not uncommon to see plus-size models, models with Down syndrome, or models with skin conditions like vitiligo all featured on the covers of magazines or used in fashion advertising.

Even Victoria's Secret, perhaps the brand most criticized for perpetuating unrealistic beauty standards over the years, announced an ambitious reinvention effort in 2021 that started with replacing the supermodel "Angels" who had come to define the brand with an inclusive group of seven pro athletes and celebrities known more for their achievements than for their body types. Six of the company's seven newly-appointed board of directors members were women, three of whom were also women of color. Time will tell if a lingerie brand that has become synonymous with a certain impossible ideal of beauty can reinvent itself . . . but their journey to do so is symbolic of the massive industry transformation happening today.

"The more we see ourselves represented in society, the more we feel like we belong in society—and the more that people who may not be a part of our groups see us as belonging in society."

▬▬▬▬▬▬ Dr. Joy Cox, Author of Fat Girls in Black Bodies

The health and fitness industry has also been evolving quickly. For years, most professional gyms and large fitness events catered to the same audience: young, good-looking, already-fit people. This bias in fitness is a familiar reality for Ragen Chastain. As a national champion dancer, two-time marathoner, and "real live fat person" (as she confidently describes herself), Chastain talks about the discrimination and condescension that she experiences at fitness events she competes in. As a "fathlete," Chastain has built a community of over 10,000 "Fit Fatties" alongside her co-founder Jeanette DePatie, and even holds the Guinness World Record for "Heaviest Woman to Complete a Marathon."

There are many other examples of diverse athletes embracing their identities with bravery and authenticity. In mid-2021, Carl Nassib became the first openly gay active NFL player. For the past eight years, a wheelchair dance team known as the Rollettes has been performing around the world, and hosting an annual gathering where hundreds of fans of all abilities celebrate their own unique identities.

Whether you consider rebranded products, shifting beauty ideals, or all types of people accepting themselves and their own bodies, there is more *identity empowerment* today than at any time in the past. The more frequently—and broadly—we see these identities humanized instead of "othered," the more possible it is to accept and embrace ourselves for who we really are.

"Pretending that we don't see race or gender is actually hurtful . . . seeing everyone as being the same actually denies people their basic human need of uniqueness."

Stefanie K. Johnson, PhD, Author of Inclusify

In an inclusive world, each of us should feel empowered to declare and explore our identities openly without fear of being ostracized for it.

What Needs To Happen . . .

Identity is the lens through which all of us experience our lives. It also shapes the way the world sees us. In the end, identity is never about "you" or "them." It is about *us*, and it is about the world we want future generations to live in.

Here are some thoughts on how we can create a world that's better—and more inclusive—than the one we're living in now.

IMPERATIVE #1

There must be more safe spaces where people of different identities can meet and engage.

You cannot understand someone whose life experience is only ever portrayed to you through movies. The best solution is to meet those "others" face-to-face. Sociologists call this experience *diversity exposure,* and it has been shown to make a difference in how willing people are to accept and respect others.[3] This is the core idea behind an initiative known as *The Human Library*.

Founded to help people learn to "unjudge someone," for the past two decades this nonprofit has hosted events where "readers can borrow human beings serving as open books and have conversations they would not normally have access to." Those who volunteer to be "borrowed" include people who are polyamorous, refugees, homeless, deafblind, or who are suffering from PTSD. Each person spends time talking candidly about their frequently misunderstood identity or situation with a stranger. The series has been wildly successful and stands as a powerful testimonial of how real conversations, whether intentionally scheduled or purely serendipitous, can open people's minds and hearts.

IMPERATIVE #2

We must support the institutions and programs that help people explore and embrace their identities.

Whether people are adjusting to an unconventional family structure or going through individual, personal, and intimate identity-altering moments, the groups supporting their journey need *our* support through funding and advocacy.

These efforts are particularly important for young people just starting out on their path of self-discovery. When we are young, it can be tempting to define ourselves through a single dimension.

"When I was growing up, there were parts of my identity that I was really struggling with. We have to go the extra mile to let kids know that whoever they are is exactly who they are meant to be."

Maulik Pancholy, Actor, Author, and Activist

Melody Lewis and Turquoise Devereaux are co-founders of the Indigenous Community Collaborative—a group that works specifically with Native American youth to help them appreciate their heritage. The challenge for Indigenous CC and other groups with similar missions remains in helping young people to understand their *intersectional* identities and find a way to be proud of them. As they shared at our summit, "We teach about a cultural spectrum . . . so no matter if you grew up on the reservation or in a city, you're still Native American."

Organizations like Indigenous CC or The Trevor Project, a non-profit that offers "life saving and life affirming services" to at-risk LGBTQ+ youth, are on the front lines of helping those struggling to understand themselves. Their work must be applauded, shared and financially supported so they can continue to help people accept and embrace their identities.

IMPERATIVE #3

Ensure legislation and corporate policy is supportive of all types of identities.

Politicians, local legislators, and corporate HR professionals all hold increased significance in the world of identity, as their work and intentions shape laws, policies, workplace practices and social norms.

When laws or policies dictate who is eligible for benefits and who isn't, or which identities don't get protection or extra support, people can be forced to see the act of embracing their identity as a personal or financial risk to be avoided or as a limiting factor rather than an empowering expression of authenticity.

The struggles of neurodiverse individuals in the workplace represent a prime example. People who are not "neurotypical" often struggle in an open-plan style office with extremely bright, fluorescent lighting and constant ambient noise. Workers in these environments may be reluctant to speak up, and instead they may choose to quietly suffer or have their work decline as a result. Corporate policy, in this case, could solve the problem by designing a sensory-friendly and more welcoming environment for all workers.

People must be guaranteed the freedom to explore, express, and bring their full selves to work without fear of reprisal or discrimination. This freedom forms the foundation for all other efforts at creating a more identity-aware and inclusive society.

What You Can Do . . .

Identity is deeply personal, as is our response to it. As a result, there are many things that any of us can do individually to help create a more inclusive world—and it starts with seeing your own identity as something that transcends any label.

The other, complementary side of this process is choosing to be more accepting of the unfamiliar identities of others. Here are several steps we can all take to accomplish both things.

Welcome conversations about identity with less judgment and more patience.

Racial anxiety is the term sociologists use to describe the fear and reluctance many of us experience when talking about anything related to race. Too many people who otherwise describe themselves as open-minded lack empathy for those who express this anxiety. Any conversation about your identity is an opportunity for you to foster more understanding in the world. But it will never happen if your first instinct is to react with outrage and judge someone instantly for asking the *wrong* question, or for unintentionally offending you.

"I think that if teenagers reached out of their circle a little bit more, we'd find that we're much more similar than we are different. And we could grow up realizing that having different perspectives doesn't mean we can't come together."

■ *Leela Ladnier, Actress & voice of Disney Junior's Mira,* *Royal Detective*

If these conversations do not happen, our culture is guaranteed to remain at a standstill. At the same time, it is also important that the emotional labor of educating others is not placed upon marginalized individuals themselves. People need to do the dual work of educating themselves *and* actively seeking out the wisdom of others, rather than passively counting on any one person to serve as a representative for an entire identity group.

For our concept of identity to be broadened and more inclusive, each of us must accept the need for a *lack of awareness* to be accepted, addressed, and handled without condemnation. Someone's ignorance about your identity may not be intended as exclusionary. It may exist simply because they have never met someone like you who was willing to engage in open dialogue with them.

ACTION #2

Use less labeling language and be more aware of how you describe or stereotype people.

Labels can easily become shorthand for how we describe people. Each of us must resist the tendency to categorize people in this limiting way. It harms their potential and creates an environment where others may feel forced to live inside a single, outside perception of who they are.

In a powerful short film created by writer and director Beecher W. Reuning titled *The Labels We Carry,* this idea of toxic labels is creatively explored as we see a man walking through his daily life literally wearing stickers with all the hurtful labels people have assigned to him. Each time someone sees and judges him, they hand him a new sticker which he attaches to his shirt. They are entirely negative. Deadbeat. Freak. Stupid. Annoying. Loser. His shirt is covered with them as he sadly goes through his daily routine.

Then, finally, someone walks past and hands him an unexpected sticker. As he puts it on, his face slowly transforms. This one says "*Loved.*" All the other stickers fall off as he walks proudly down the street with his head held high.[4]

As the man passes a stranger, he offers another sticker with the same message to him. As the scene fades, we see that stranger's face transform, too.

 Watch *The Labels We Carry* short film at www.nonobviousdiversity.com/resources

Imagine if you could go through just one day offering this type of validation to everyone you encountered. Unfortunately, many times we may thoughtlessly do the exact opposite. What judgments did you make about the last person who cut you off in traffic? Or the person near you who was speaking too loudly on their mobile phone in public?

We all have daily moments where we might practice more empathy and understanding for those around us instead of defining them with labels. We just need to choose to do so.

"We don't say 'differing abilities,' that's a phrase that non-disabled people made up to make themselves feel comfortable. It's much more important that we all recognize and respect the rights of people with disabilities."

━━━━━ Rebecca Cokley, American Disability Rights Advocate

━━━━ ACTION #3 ━━━━

Lean into the intersections of your own identity and become a role model.

When each of us becomes comfortable with the numerous layers of our own identities, we not only find fulfillment for ourselves, but we can also serve as an example for the people around us. In 2007 Waylon Pahona Jr. was close to rock bottom, contemplating suicide. A Hopi and Tewa/Maricopa who grew up on the Hopi reservation, Waylon had been abused at age 9, saved his mother from attempted suicide at the age of 16 and struggled with weight his entire life.

It was fitness that transformed Pahona's life, and today he is the founder of a group called Healthy Active Natives (HANs) that has helped more than 75,000 fellow Natives get healthier. As a rare Native American voice in the world of fitness, Pahona feels a deep sense of responsibility as a role model not only for his community, but for his two sons who will grow up with a far different relationship with their father than he had with his.

"I've come to realize that identity is meant to be multidimensional in order for it to teach acceptance and tolerance. We all have the power to change our fate from karmic (doomed to repeat itself) to dharmic (emancipation from life and death). It starts with belonging to yourself instead of to others."

Raj Girn, Founder, Anokhi Life & The Open Chest Confidence Academy

By learning about and embracing your own unique identity and sharing it with others, you can become a sorely needed role model for other people.

Beyond Diversity In
IDENTITY

🏛 WHAT NEEDS TO HAPPEN:

- ❯ There must be more safe spaces where people of different identities can meet and engage.

- ❯ We must support the institutions and programs that help people explore and embrace their identities.

- ❯ Ensure legislation and corporate policy is supportive of all types of identities.

WHAT *YOU* CAN DO:

- ❯ Welcome conversations about identity with less judgment and more patience.

- ❯ Use less labeling language and be more aware of how you describe or stereotype people.

- ❯ Lean into the intersections of your own identity and become a role model.

💬 CONVERSATION STARTERS:

- ❯ Write 3-5 sentences describing your identity. How have those words changed over time?

- ❯ What is one conversation or activity that you could engage in to better understand an identity different from your own?

BEYOND DIVERSITY IN
FAMILY

"The diversity in the human family should be the cause of love and harmony, as it is in music where many different notes blend together in the making of a perfect chord."

— *'Abdu'l-Bahá, Former Head of the Bahá'í Faith*

Chapter Summary:

The notion of family has evolved dramatically. A rise in biracial marriages, same-sex unions, multi-generational households, intentionally childless couples, caregivers and stepfamilies are all signs of this shift. Yet workplace inequity and cultural pressures remain. To change this, we must update policies, shift cultural norms, and become more individually accepting of family structures different from our own.

How It Is . . .

In April of 2018, *National Geographic* magazine devoted their entire monthly issue to the topic of race. The cover featured a portrait of two 11-year-old biracial fraternal twins named Marcia and Millie Biggs. Born to interracial parents, Millie has darker skin, brown eyes and black hair. Her sister Marcia has light skin, blue eyes and blonde hair.

Despite their shared upbringing, the twins were routinely treated very differently by strangers they encountered—as were their parents, depending on which one they were with. The twins challenged people's deeply held beliefs about race, and at the same time shattered traditional conventions regarding the racial makeup of families.

The fact is these conventions have quickly become outdated. According to Pew Research, one in seven babies born in the US today is multiracial or multiethnic.[1] In Sweden's three biggest cities (Stockholm, Gothenburg, and Malmö), more than *half* of children under 18 have one parent who was born outside of Sweden.[2]

There has been a steep rise in stepfamilies as well. The US Census Bureau reports that one in two marriages ends in divorce, and over 50 percent of US families are remarried or re-coupled. In some nations like Australia, estimates suggest nearly 20 percent of all families might fall into this category.[3]

The numbers of same-sex couples with and without children, people who remain single, and couples who stay childless either by choice or circumstance are also all on the rise.

If there is one clear conclusion to take from all this demographic data, it is that the concept of *family* itself is shifting. The trend raises a fundamental question that will shape our exploration throughout this chapter: *what is a family?*

At the height of the post-World War II baby boom in 1960, most people's answer to this question was relatively straightforward. Seventy-three percent of all children in the US were living in a family with two married parents of the same ethnicity in their first marriage.[4] Two generations later, families might consist of parents who are divorced, single, remarried, and/or cohabitating, as well as grandparents or other family members raising kids, older siblings and foster families.

Families are also multi-generational, with caregivers frequently providing for older or disabled family members. According to Pew Research Center, one in five Americans lives in a household with multiple generations under one roof. Globally, this ratio in many countries is far higher where family members of varying generations living together is the norm.

This fluidity has led to a reimagining of how we understand the concept of family, and the word "family" has come to be more reflective of an individual's reality and circumstances at different moments throughout their lives, rather than at birth or specific life milestones such as marriage.

In the past, a family might also have been described as an insular unit with a male father and a female mother. This too has changed. The legalization of same-sex marriage in 29 countries around the world (as of the time of this writing) and the queer community's well-established notion of "chosen family" has led to a vastly more diverse combination of domestic structures, proving that *family* is an ever-changing idea.

7% of all newlyweds were in an interracial marriage in 1980, and by 2015, that share had more than doubled to 17%.

Source: Pew Research, 2017

Despite the growing evidence of this evolution of family structures, there continues to be a societal bias toward the "traditional" family structure which includes persistent expectations about the role that mothers and fathers are assumed to take in childrearing. Women may be more than half the workforce in many countries, but research shows that they are still expected to take the primary role in childcare.

In contrast, fathers are often judged as incapable of providing responsible parenting despite the reality that in many cultures, fathers are more involved today than at any other time in the past.

Yet the most common discrimination against parents in the workplace continues to affect mothers, who are often hindered by perceptions that they can't balance the division of time between work and family.

These beliefs concerning what a "typical" family is and the roles male and female parents or caregivers ought to take in it have led to entrenched biases in our culture and workplaces. One clear example is the inequity of parental and caregiver leave policies that are inconsistently offered at workplaces around the world.

In many companies, if paid leave is offered at all, it is offered solely to the mother who gives birth to the child. Adoptive parents, stepparents, and fathers are largely ignored, even though each is experiencing the same life-changing moment of becoming a parent. This creates a double-bias: against the birth parent, who is largely expected to prioritize childcare over career; and against the non-birth parent(s), who are treated as less important to the child's development.

There also continues to be widespread prejudice against the growing number of families who remain childless either by circumstance or choice, and against single people who choose not to marry or have children. In her eye-opening book *Otherhood*, author Melanie Notkin explores the lives of women of childbearing age who

6 in 10 childless women are voluntarily childless.

Source: Statistics Netherlands

are not mothers. Notkin exposes the persistent cultural pressure and expectation that every woman must attach her self-worth to the experience of motherhood.

The bottom line is, as family units across the world are changing in composition, diversity, and needs, our most stubborn conventions—whether in spheres of government, career, or everyday culture—must change alongside them.

How Things Are Changing . . .

In 2011 Jordan Thierry spent two years exploring a big question about Black fatherhood. How could he counter common media stereotypes of Black fathers in defense of involved fathers like his own?[5]

The mission to share the real stories of Black families led Thierry on a journey to release his first documentary film in 2013, titled *The Black Fatherhood Project*. In it, he explores the myths and realities of Black fatherhood, and spotlights the belief that creating a more inclusive world also means expanding our definition of families to include those who step in to help. To this point, his second film, *Grandma's Roses*, focuses on the central and courageous roles that women elders of color often play in families as "centerpieces and culture-keepers."

As a Venezuelan American immigrant and successful pediatrician, Dr. Edith Bracho-Sanchez learned from her patients about the importance of family, and how that term is not limited to people with whom you share a genetic identity. Sometimes the term can be used to describe people who step up and offer their love and support, even though they may not be related by blood.

Reliable adults—related or not—who step up to help a child in need *are* family, and anyone who has had an adoptive parent, stepsibling, or who has otherwise benefitted from the kindness and love of an unrelated person would agree. Yet even as our definition of family undergoes rapid changes, the development of systems and support that allows non-blood relatives to more easily provide for and nurture loved ones has been happening at a much slower pace.

Beyond the way we describe family to one another or perceive it ourselves, the way family is defined and supported by governments and corporate entities must also become more equitable and inclusive. Many progressive companies are leading the way by instituting transparent and equitable parental leave policies, gender-neutral benefits, support for caregivers, and flexible working hours.[6]

In addition to corporate-led initiatives such as these, there are many nonprofit groups and independent community organizers who are offering resources to help modern families succeed in parenting *and* achieving a reasonable work-life balance by evolving their workplaces to be more family friendly.

Jessica DeGroot, founder of the ThirdPath Institute, believes another aspect of the solution is to have a candid conversation about shared parenting even before becoming parents. "I'm asking couples before they become too exhausted to think differently, to ignore all their neighbors, colleagues, family members, and these cultural norms," she shares, "and to start to imagine their own way." This way—which she calls the "third path"—is grounded in authentic dialogue between partners, encouraging them to create time and energy for both aspects of their lives—work and family.

Another example is Soy Super Papá, an online community founded by Sergio Alejandro Rosario with the mission of empowering fathers by highlighting their roles in society and offering them resources and support.

The community provides dads with a safe space to share experiences, and aims to foster a healthier culture of active fatherhood in every society. There has been a similarly supportive movement in recent years specifically aimed at supporting the fatherhood journey for gay dads.

To continue this momentum, a few critical puzzle pieces need to fall into place sooner rather than later.

What Needs To Happen...

In the future, a one-dimensional portrait of a family will no longer be the prevailing one. Instead, families will be increasingly multi-ethnic, multi-generational, childless by choice, and not limited to heterosexual couples or those in married relationships.

To build a more inclusive world, we must move toward building more accommodations into our modern workplaces for all types of families, and more acceptance into our social fabric for neighbors and colleagues who live in family structures different than our own.

Here are some priorities we will need to address and actions we must take along the way.

IMPERATIVE #1

We must create an equitable workplace that helps every worker balance family and work.

Cultural perceptions surrounding professional success routinely portray the ideal worker as a person who arrives early, leaves late, and makes everything in life secondary to their career.

This admiration of overwork, often called "hustle," continues to be celebrated as a key ingredient of success. Consequently, when many "non-dominant" parents try to take time for family activities, they are judged for lacking commitment to their careers. Rohit recounts a moment that may feel familiar to many fathers, when he was leaving work early to attend a parent-teacher meeting. The looks from his male colleagues seemed to wonder: "why can't your wife handle that?" The unfairness of this attitude affects everyone involved.

To combat this not-so-subtle judgment, and create a more equitable work environment, change must start at the top. Are the most senior leaders of all genders in a company prioritizing life events on their work calendar, and advocating this amongst their teams? The examples they set trickle down throughout their organizations in powerful ways.

As Leslie Forde, founder of the Mom's Hierarchy of Needs Framework rightfully points out, "The culture of always being available barely worked when we were captive in the office. And it doesn't translate to remote work. People can't be on call for meetings until five or six o'clock at night. Parents are burning out . . . but they are also terrified of losing their jobs. So often they won't speak up or tell you they're vulnerable."

Employers have to be proactive in supporting a flexible and family friendly workplace that allows people to be parents and caregivers, as well as employees.

Organizations must create and fund programs that proactively support caregivers and parents.

At work, many companies have begun formalizing parent & caregiver employee resource groups (ERGs). These forward-thinking organizations have realized that workers who feel supported at home are better able to do their best thinking at work—even when work and home occupy the same space in a society where many people have been forced to work remotely, and where even more are now actively choosing to work this way.

For both types of workers, large organizations across many industries—including Bank of America, Novartis, IBM, and many others—are all investing in family-related support programs for caregivers and parents alike.

Both groups must believe they have the safety to speak up if they feel their experience is not being respected. This is particularly important when it comes to the experiences of caregivers because they can vary widely. Some may be caring for a disabled child while others may be tending to an ailing parent. Some may even have both.

21.3% of Americans have provided care to an adult or child with special needs in the past 12 months.

Source: AARP Caregiving Report 2020

Creating a workplace that is welcoming of the needs of these families requires flexibility and empathy. In addition to ERGs, organizations must make sure to create a work culture that is respectful of teammates who need to leave work at a very specific time (or stop work hours if they are working remotely) and those who may ask for materials to be shared virtually so they can remain connected and deliver tasks on time by working outside typical business hours.

Lawmakers need to pass legislation requiring more support for parents and caregivers.

There are widespread global differences in how supportive governments are towards the needs of families. For example, many Scandinavian countries provide considerable federal resources for new parents that seem extreme in comparison to other nations.

The parental or caregiver support available in certain countries, including the United States, is far less than what is offered in most other developed nations. Of the world's wealthiest countries, the US is one of only a handful that does not guarantee any maternity or paternity leave.

By contrast, many countries around the globe offer generous paid leave for both parents, regardless of gender, and regardless of whether they are biological parents or adoptive ones. Estonia, for example, offers over a year and a half of paid leave to new parents, making it one of the most supportive nations in the world when it comes to family rights and health.

Though paid parental leave is usually connected to a country's specific economic and political structures, the message still stands: governments and lawmakers need to act more purposefully to ease the burdens placed on working parents and caregivers.

What You Can Do . . .

Family is a complex and deeply personal concept that is unique to every person, but there are certain benchmarks we can all strive to achieve in the pursuit of widespread equity and inclusion in the workplace and in our culture.

Here are some tips for how to do this yourself.

ACTION #1

Welcome more conversations about family in the workplace from all team members.

In a professional setting, many women are accustomed to questions about their families and children. As a result, they can simultaneously be more comfortable with bringing their alternate identities as mothers or caregivers into the workplace than men.

Men who are fathers or caregivers, on the other hand, may struggle with the same expectations for opposite reasons. They are rarely asked about their kids or family and therefore feel reluctant to bring them up at all. While women can feel limited by assumptions or judgments about how their family life affects their job performance, men feel that their fatherhood or relationship with their family is irrelevant at work. And then there are non-binary or agender people who don't identify with any of these traditional gender-based parenting labels, yet still may be a parent, or a caregiver, or responsible for meeting other non-traditional family obligations.

If we want people to bring their whole selves into work, we must make it acceptable for anyone and everyone to talk about and share their family experience—and we must also ensure that people don't feel judged or excluded if they are neither a caregiver nor a parent.

------------------------- ACTION #2 -------------------------

Be more compassionate with your loved ones who struggle to accept non-traditional families.

As families grow more diverse, we're likely to encounter relatives and friends who are less accepting of family structures they don't understand.

Dr. David Campt, aptly nicknamed The Dialogue Guy, says that leaning into these interactions with understanding is the best way to go about inspiring change: "People will listen to you more if you listen to them first. How do you listen to them first? You ask questions."

His belief, supported by years of helping deal with difficult conversations, is if we lead with compassion in mind, we can move even the most reluctant people to accept and even understand family structures unlike their own.

ACTION #3

Broaden our depictions of family in every situation, from media and entertainment to school curricula.

Imagining how we might build a more inclusive world for all types of families will also require each of us to bring together many of the themes that have been explored in other chapters of this book.

For example, we need to reimagine how our schools teach children about the concept of family, and what it really means to different people. At work, we must fix the inherent gender-based biases that reinforce traditional parenting roles instead of helping modern families to evolve and succeed.

The stories we share must integrate the stories of more nontraditional families and portray them through media and entertainment as normal and authentic. And, of course, we must respect that each of our identities—and those held by others—are deeply shaped by the family dynamics that we have at home right now, as well as the ones we grew up with in the past.

Our families are linked to who we are, but they are sometimes made invisible in our interactions at work and in public. The only way to build a world more inclusive of different types of family structures is to engage in conversations about them and choose to be more welcoming of all types of familial structures, particularly those different from your own.

Beyond Diversity In
FAMILY

🏛 WHAT NEEDS TO HAPPEN:

- We must create an equitable workplace that helps every worker balance family and work.
- Organizations must create and fund programs that proactively support caregivers and parents.
- Lawmakers need to pass legislation requiring more support for parents and caregivers.

WHAT *YOU* CAN DO:

- Welcome more conversations about family in the workplace from all team members.
- Be more compassionate with your loved ones who struggle to accept non-traditional families.
- Broaden our depictions of family in every situation, from media and entertainment to school curricula.

💬 CONVERSATION STARTERS:

- How much of your home life do you feel comfortable sharing at work and why do you feel this way?
- Where do you see diversity in your own family and how would you define diversity?
- What values were you taught by your family members, and which ones did you develop on your own?

BEYOND DIVERSITY IN
CULTURE

"It often takes a meal to penetrate a culture and see how similar we all are. The world would be a better place if we thought more about the things that bring us together rather than separate us."
— *Chef José Andrés*

Chapter Summary:

Culture is everything from what we believe to the things we are passionate about. To build a more inclusive world for all cultures, we must find new ways for dominant cultures and subcultures—based on individual passions or identities—to co-exist, sometimes blend, and never be used for exclusion or discrimination.

How It Is . . .

If you are an English speaker, you already know that a dog goes *woof*. But in Spanish, dogs say *guau*. In Japanese, it's *wan*. And in Turkish, dogs go *hav*. In 2015 a British illustrator named James Chapman decided to publish a book exploring these linguistic quirks—*How To Sneeze In Japanese*.

Indulging his fascination with international onomatopoeia, he explores how the sound of a sneeze (*atchim* in Portuguese) or a cough (*khau* in Punjabi) or a yawn (*hao* in Thai) varies across the globe. Traveling around the world, you will find a similar variety in the way that humans greet each other from one region to the next.

In São Paulo, it is customary to greet one another with one *beijo*—where you touch your right cheek to the person you're greeting. In Rio de Janeiro, it's *dois beijos*—two kisses. In India, they use folded hands—*namaste*. Japan has bows. Sometimes these learned behaviors can be different within the same country as well. In a now viral video from 2012, former US President Barack Obama greets a White basketball coach with a traditional handshake right before dapping up Black basketball star Kevin Durant.

Body language and gestures, too, vary widely. Across Asia, the beckoning sign is always given to someone with the palm facing down. In America, it is palm facing up. There are hundreds of examples of these sorts of traditions and practices that distinguish cultures from one another.

The most common definition of culture describes it as patterns of learned and shared behaviors and beliefs across a certain group. More interesting, though, is what people sometimes choose to elevate in the way they define culture. For some, culture is all about language and traditions. For others, it is about beliefs and values. Sometimes, it can even be something as straightforward as the words we use to describe the sound of a sneeze.

Culture encompasses many parts of our lives—from the things we are passionate about to the stories we find funny or offensive. Perhaps unsurprisingly, it is why we so often see the word used in conjunction with another. *Geek culture* and *sneaker culture* are just two examples of thousands of such terms people use to describe culture based on what they love. Terms like *queer culture* or *deaf culture* are used to describe cultures based on identities. *Corporate culture* is commonly used in the professional world for a shared set of beliefs at work. A *counterculture* is one whose values oppose those of mainstream society. A *subculture* is a smaller cultural group within a larger one.

All of these ways of describing culture illustrate a fundamental truth that will frame this chapter. Our culture is not only based on the language we speak or the region we live in or the food we eat or the way we describe our identity. It is not only the place we work or the faith we choose or the stories we believe. Culture is *all* these things together, and an inclusive world is one where all of us are free to belong to the cultures we choose without being judged for our choices.

Unfortunately, this type of cultural acceptance can feel hard to imagine given how divergent some cultural beliefs can be. For example, in mid-2021 the Pew Research Center released a telling survey that asked respondents whether they felt "people are too easily offended by what others say." The answers were sharply divided between those on the political left and those on the right with an unprecedented gap of 42 points between them. The depth of these beliefs has even been described as a "culture war" that can feel impossible to change.

50% to 90% of the world's languages are predicted to disappear by the next century.

Source: UNESCO Atlas of the World's Languages in Danger

The truth is, for much of human history different cultures have not always happily co-existed. Instead, dominant cultures have consistently destroyed other cultures along their way to becoming dominant. Consider the heartbreaking death of languages. According to joint research from the National Geographic Society and the Living Tongues Institute for Endangered Languages, there are nearly 7000 languages spoken in the world today, and experts worry that *nearly half* are in danger of extinction. A third of the world's languages are estimated to have fewer than 1,000 speakers left, and every two weeks a language dies with its last speaker.

At the same time, the world's most dominant languages are getting even more dominant. By some estimates, nearly 2 billion people across the world speak English today. Some historians logically attribute this to the aggressiveness of British colonization over hundreds of years. Cultural experts suggest the spread of both the language and American culture comes from the "soft power" exerted by America's robust music and film industries that provide content to the world.

An even more personal example is the relatively common practice among some immigrant communities of abandoning their ethnic birth names and adopting locally popular names to better fit into the culture of their adopted homes. When a language dies or people feel pressured to change their names to fit in, another piece of global diversity disappears.

The global exporting of traditional Western ideals of family, relationships, and identity keeps them firmly at the center of pop (popular) culture. In response, people have developed unique coping mechanisms to blend their own cultures with the one they often see represented in films and television. And they have started subcultures to rebel against the mainstream and redefine themselves and shift culture around them in the process.

This is the paradox at the heart of our modern culture. There are simultaneous forces that subsume other cultures, traditions and languages and emerging culture wars between people with differing worldviews even as there are global movements rising up to keep those same unique cultures and beliefs alive.

"If you're doing something outside of dominant culture, there's not an easy place for you. You will have to do it yourself."

Ava DuVernay, American Filmmaker

As a result, many affected people develop a unique portfolio of different behaviors, communication styles, and language to signal their belonging in multiple cultures. This could be looked at as a painful compromise and extra labor we do to fit in, or as an intentional strategy that enables people to inhabit multiple cultures at once. *Code switching* (also referred to as covering or masking) is a common way of describing the way some people have become adept at changing their language, mannerisms, style of speech or expressions to blend in with the dominant culture. Jennifer regularly advises senior leaders on the impact of code switching or covering and how employees may do this in anticipation of being negatively stereotyped. They don't speak up out of fear of reprisal of having their career derailed. Covering too brings an emotional tax, insidiously diminishing a person's identity and keeping them from being seen and heard.

Sociologist, historian, and writer W. E. B. Dubois famously writes about the concept of "double consciousness" in his 1903 book, *The Souls of Black Folk*. He describes the phenomenon as an awareness of always being judged through the eyes of others. What code switching often reveals are situations where people don't feel like they can truly be themselves.

For example, one study from a team of researchers from Harvard, Cornell and the University of Michigan found that in some professional circumstances, it can be a strategic way to try and fit in but carries with it significant psychological costs.[1] When people feel there is no way for cultures to co-exist, our shared diversity suffers.

"Culture is never the whole of any answer. It is always—along with economics, politics, one's genes, one's neighborhood, one's times, and more—only a part. It is way too easy to use culture to support stereotypes."

Gish Jen, Author of The Girl at the Baggage Claim

NPR journalist Gene Demby, creator of the *Code Switch* podcast, describes this dance as a daily "hop-scotching between different cultural and linguistic spaces and different parts of our own identities."[2]

This optimistic perspective suggests that we can have it all, inhabiting our primary and secondary cultures proudly while connecting to and acknowledging others'. What are the inadvertent strengths and competencies that people use to do this, and what is the right balance between code switching and authenticity? This is just one of the big questions that is shaping our exploration of how culture is shifting.

How Things Are Changing . . .

In the 1950s, an American husband-wife duo of sociologists named John and Ruth Useem were living in India with their three children. Seeking a way to describe the experience of their family living and working abroad, they coined the term "third culture kids" (TCK).

Decades later researchers Paulette Bethel and Ruth E. Van Reken suggested that these TCKs develop a worldview that is "not readily apparent on the outside, unlike the usual diversity markers such as race, ethnicity, nationality and so on." Under this view, these third culture kids weren't so much culturally rootless as they were *inventing* their own unique "third" culture. The very notion of a third culture kid presents an intriguing example of how culture isn't something that only exists in silos. At the same time, the term has been criticized for perpetuating a so-called "hierarchy of foreignness" that portrays one culture as superior to another.

"Preservation of one's own culture does not require contempt or disrespect for other cultures."

Cesar Chavez, American Civil Rights Activist

As we consider how culture itself is evolving, we can start with the images in the media and marketing that are often used to visualize culture—and the company that has supplied most of them.

Getty Images is the world's leading supplier of stock images, editorial photography, video and music for business and consumers, with an archive of over 200 million assets. With such a monopoly on global visual culture, Getty Images has also long recognized their responsibility to create diverse and inclusive imagery. Over the past decade in particular, the brand has risen to the challenge by partnering with various groups and organizations to create custom sets of images.

The Disability Collection, supported by Verizon Media, includes a growing library of images that more authentically portray individuals with disabilities. In Project #ShowUs, Dove and Girlgaze partnered to create a collection of 14,000+ photographs devoted to shattering stereotypical beauty standards. The Nosotros Collection shifts visual representation of the Latinx/ Hispanic community using images and video to tell stories through the community's own voice. When the imagery we see offers a differing perspective on culture and identity, it can have a transformative effect.

 See our Non-Obvious Diversity Collection curated in partnership with Getty Images at www.nonobviousdiversity.com/resources

Claudia Marks, Senior Art Director of Getty Images, says initiatives like these speak to the organization's mission to move hearts, minds, opinions, and societal perceptions while offering an arsenal of positive imagery for retail companies (and many others) to use. "We try to be more proactive in offering up the kinds of content we want to see; in showing the kind of world we want to live in. We think about intersectionality, we think about making sure our images are true and reflective of identity. We think about diversity and inclusion above and beyond race."

Alongside these sorts of inclusive image collections, the hybridization of language also offers an example of how diverse cultures are starting to co-exist more deeply. Nearly 350 million people in China have some knowledge of English, as do another 100 million or more in India.[3] When added to the millions of people across Europe, Africa and Latin America who also speak English, there are more people who speak some form of English across the world than in predominantly English-speaking nations (another outcome of the "language death" discussed earlier). And because so many people speak English as their second or third language, hybrid forms are emerging. *Hinglish*, *Spanglish*, and *Chinglish* are already widely used terms from diverse communities that describe how their English is something different from the mainstream.

Whether through the lived experience of third culture kids, the evolution of inclusive imagery, or the hybridization of our language, the theme that emerges is that culture is an ever-changing thing that continually reflects the beliefs, passions, and experiences of all of us as we shape it. Culture is neither good nor bad, but it can be used as a tool to exclude people, or to bring people together. What will it take for us to build a more inclusive culture that allows for these different experiences to not just co-exist but be truly valued, celebrated and transformed through a mixing of cultures into something unprecedented and unique?

What Needs To Happen...

The journey toward crafting a more inclusive shared culture is one that touches many subjects. The food we enjoy, the jokes we find funny, the films we spend time watching are all examples of ways we engage with the culture around us. In our summit, we took a wide-ranging view of culture, which you can see reflected in the range of sessions we hosted on the topic. These conversations illuminated some key priorities that must be achieved for all institutions and industries to move toward true cultural inclusion.

IMPERATIVE #1

We must celebrate examples of a global view of citizenship that honors humanity above nationality.

The musical group Now United is beloved by millions of fans across the world. The creation of American Idol co-founder Simon Fuller, the music group brings together 17 singers and dancers from all different nations. Together they produce catchy pop songs and offer an irresistibly young, optimistic and inclusive vision of the future. As group project manager Yonta Taiwo explains: "It's about accepting each other's differences and inspiring one another through music and dance. After all, music is the universal language!"

In music videos from the group, you can see each member wearing the flag of their respective country even as they unite as artists. The moments of global unity like this are relatively few. Sometimes we experience this at the Olympic Games, or through entertainers like Now United, but in order to promote a more inclusive culture, we all need to seek out and share more examples like these and remind ourselves that being a global citizen means appreciating our shared humanity no matter what nation someone might call home.

IMPERATIVE #2

Institutions must embrace culturally inclusive conversations instead of avoiding difficult questions.

Much of what we learn of culture is taught through school history lessons and reinforced by the stories we hear in the communities and cultures in which we are raised. When significant historical moments are minimized or avoided, our shared understanding of culture becomes warped. At our summit, cultural historian Marisa Brown shared that "students come wanting to go out and change their fields, museum practice, preservation, and heritage studies. They see the problems of White dominance and supremacy in the history of these institutions, and they are really committed to making lasting changes."

Instead of seeing our past as an opportunity to learn from our mistakes and do better, when we refuse to discuss it, we doom ourselves to repeating the same mistakes. Instead, institutions of all sorts must find a way to bring conversations about culture into their spaces and encourage those who wish to study it. For example, Dr. Ayana Omilade Flewellen teaches a course on African Diaspora Archeology at the University of California, Riverside. She shares a story of how her students get excited about discovering this area of study:

"My job right now is really centered around introducing students to a new avenue in which they can engage with African diaspora history through material culture [and] it's the first time that they've seen a Black woman who does this work or critically asked themselves questions about their own heritage."

IMPERATIVE #3

Media companies, news outlets, and creators of content must work to reflect a more accurate portrayal of culture.

Many people experience life in a cultural bubble, only interacting with the people in their hometowns and neighboring communities. If not culturally diverse, a person's understanding of others will be heavily influenced by what they see in media and news outlets. Selective coverage that only highlight small, stereotypical cultural tropes are no longer acceptable.

"People don't know very much about Native American people. I use that as a weapon in my comedy. Our job as comedians is to shine a light on weird things that are happening in the world and sometimes share these uncomfortable truths that people aren't ready to hear."

Joey Clift, Television Writer and Comedian

Media companies and news outlets must invest in more culturally diverse talent who can help tell stories from authentic experiences, and who can recognize flawed representations of people and places. When representation is missing, as we first shared in the chapter on Storytelling, the stories told do not reflect the reality of today's cultures and identities, making it difficult to see where there are universal human truths.

What You Can Do . . .

In a summit discussion centered on Muslim representation in media and entertainment, poet, TV/film producer and writer Amir Sulaiman recalls being called in as an advisor and eventually cast as an actor in the hit Hulu show *Ramy*. When first asked for his perspective as a Black Muslim Sufi, his priority was to represent people authentically: "Nothing is perfect, but as best as we can we have at least an authentic representation of these men and women that I know from my community."

His experience offers insight into the importance of listening to the perspective of those from inside of a particular culture. Let's consider some ways to do this that we might all individually practice.

Reassess your cultural fluency in the workplace.

Cultural fluency—or the ability to understand people from different cultural backgrounds—is a critical skill for every one of us. Not only is it essential for building trust and empathy in multicultural workplaces, but it has been repeatedly linked to enhanced financial performance.[4] Leaders can start by trying to practice more *cultural humility* by stepping out of their own experiences to identify their knowledge gaps about other cultures. Then leaders must take the next step to broaden their knowledge through seeking exposure to different media, content, and diversifying their personal networks. Eventually, they must evolve to become a champion for more complete cultural representation.

The need to navigate these nuances for those who must interact with people from different parts of the world has given rise to an entire industry of intercultural experts. Their existence offers an insight into how we often think about culture itself. There is even a now-decades-old guide called *Kiss, Bow or Shake Hands* that offers a 600-page country-by-country breakdown of culturally appropriate "do's and don'ts" for doing business anywhere.

. . . IN CULTURE   89

Cultural fluency takes more than learning the top five "do's and don'ts" for every country or culture. Instead, the people who are observant about the way that those from other cultures or backgrounds communicate can not only build bridges between cultures, but be instrumental in creating more opportunities for collaboration and understanding among those from different backgrounds.

ACTION #2

Be willing to learn about other cultural traditions and support ambitious alliances.

Food is perhaps the most accessible way to experience another culture. It does not require you to have a friend or colleague from another culture and you don't even need to travel outside your hometown. In tasting food from other cultures, we are reminded that there are different lives that exist outside of our own. Chicago-based Indian cookbook author Anupy Singla described the power of cuisine to open people's minds about different cultures during a session on food at our summit:

"From all of my classes and demos, I find the day-to-day person is incredibly open to new ideas, new tastes, new recipes. I start by saying 'There are no bad questions.' I think once you take that pressure off, it truly opens doors because people love to share culture through food."

Anupy Singla, Cookbook Author and Journalist

The personal journey each of us may take to appreciate different cultures can also be fundamentally shaped by those who are willing to lead a movement to break down the barriers that sometimes keep cultures apart. People like Father Jim Martin. As a Jesuit priest, Father Martin has worked to bring the identity-driven cultures of Catholicism and the LGBTQ+ community closer together. His 2018 book *Building a Bridge* offers a roadmap for how these two cultures might co-exist.

Many companies are also embracing religion in the workplace —something that used to be taboo. One corporation has established employee affinity groups around three of the religions represented in the workplace: Muslim, Christian, and Jewish.

What's interesting is how these three groups collaborate and work together. They regularly host faith-based roundtable forums to discuss religious differences—and similarities. The discussions focused on building bridges and a greater understanding of all religions, and how to have respectful, spiritual conversations across cultural boundaries, even if you have different faiths.

Another initiative pairs up employees in groups to visit area churches, synagogues, and mosques for a first-hand experience of different expressions of faith. Employees that participated in these visits learned they actually had more in common than they thought. As they find commonality, they form more cohesive, productive teams.

While food and religion may seem like wildly divergent topics, the lesson behind both of these examples is that cultures can co-exist effectively if we are willing to rethink our perspectives about what keeps them apart in the first place.

━━━━━ **ACTION #3** ━━━━━

Participate in subcultures that you love and do what it takes to make them more inclusive.

In 2020, University of Illinois Professor Kishonna Gray, a researcher who had long studied "race, gender, and deviance" in the gaming industry, published a book about multiple cultures coming together. The new book was called *Intersectional Tech* and explored the experience of Black gamers. It was a book that spotlighted a part of the gaming community that was used to being ignored and sometimes harassed.

> "Playing games as a black, queer gamer and as a woman . . . I can find a space where other people are like me, where they speak my language and where they understand my culture. We've been connecting in virtual spaces for a really long time."
>
> ━━━━━━ *Melissa Boone, Senior Xbox Research Manager*

Kate Sánchez, creator of the popular gaming news platform But Why Tho? echoed this same experience, sharing the importance of telling the stories of the subculture of gamers in a more inclusive way because often gaming and gamers themselves are stereotypically described in a way that doesn't usually include women, non-binary gamers or people of color.

Addressing another routinely ignored segment of the gaming industry is a platform called Can I Play That? created by gamer Courtney Craven. Their goal has been to influence the gaming industry to create more accessible ways for people with all sorts of disabilities to play games.

Taken together, the efforts of these pioneers in gaming illustrate the perfect model for creating an inclusive culture. If all these groups can work together, appreciate one another, and support the thing they all love, there is hope that we might all accomplish this same result with other aspects of our global culture.

Beyond Diversity In
CULTURE

🏛 WHAT NEEDS TO HAPPEN:

- We must celebrate examples of a global view of citizenship that honors humanity above nationality.
- Institutions must embrace culturally inclusive conversations instead of avoiding difficult questions.
- Media companies, news outlets, and creators of content must work to reflect a more accurate portrayal of culture.

WHAT *YOU* CAN DO:

- Reassess your cultural fluency in the workplace.
- Be willing to learn about other cultural traditions and support ambitious alliances.
- Participate in subcultures that you love and do what it takes to make them more inclusive.

💬 CONVERSATION STARTERS:

- How was culture discussed in your home growing up or in your school? What was missing?
- How do you feel about the idea of being a global citizen, and what does this mean to you?
- List 2-3 cultures or subcultures you know nothing about. Now go and discover one new fact about each one.

BEYOND DIVERSITY IN
EDUCATION

"In my view, no subject is ever finished.
Knowledge is continuous; ideas flow. I like to
imagine a world where no matter where you are
born . . . you're able to tap into your potential."

— **Sal Khan, Founder of Khan Academy**

Chapter Summary:

*What we teach, how it is presented, and who is teaching all
play a critical role in how students understand the world.
Shielding them from the truth of history or shying away
from difficult topics does not prepare students for reality.
Instead, we must reassess our school systems and curricula
to teach youth how to thrive in a diverse world.*

How It Is . . .

When Priya Vulchi and Winona Guo were 15-year-old sophomores at a public high school in New Jersey, the topic of race came up in one of their classes. It was the first time that either of them, even as Asian American students, had been confronted with the subject in school.

As central as race is to how human history has unfolded, it was noticeably absent from the core curriculum of their public school system.

Winona and Priya's experience was not unique. Finding the right way to talk to students of all ages about complex social topics or the history of issues such as racism or genocide is a daunting challenge. This question has generated intense debates among parents, educators, and students themselves.

For some, the logical answer is to teach the brutal truth of history to children without filters. Others believe children should be protected from such harsh truths, particularly when they are young. The lack of consensus on this issue has resulted in school systems that continue to struggle with addressing diversity, equity and inclusion issues related to systemic racism and societal disparities in the classroom and integrating them into lesson plans.

To tackle the issue directly, Priya and Winona decided to take action. In 2014, they co-founded the nonprofit organization

CHOOSE to develop and share racial literacy tools and curricula for educators and students to integrate effective dialogue about race into the school system.

Their goal is to establish racial literacy as a modern-day life skill—one that they hope becomes commonplace among the next generation.

Of course, racial literacy is just one of the many lenses we might apply to the topic of diversity, inclusion, and equity in education. Equity in access to education itself remains an urgent worldwide dilemma. Globally, the world's poorest children are "four times more likely not to go to school than the world's richest children, and five times more likely not to complete primary school."[1]

69% of Black eighth-grade students attend schools where a majority of students are people of color.

SOURCE: Economic Policy Institute

Segregation and division within educational systems persist as well. We continue to see racially divided school populations, barriers to educating girls in many developing nations, and a generational lack of social integration among students from different ethnicities, even within schools that do have diverse student populations.

This segregation happens along economic lines also, adding to the depressing reality that for many people, the zip code or town they were raised in continues to dictate everything from their education to their career prospects to their overall life expectancy.[2]

This underscores a sobering reality. Avoiding a gradual re-segregation of schools will require immediate action on multiple fronts, including how governments set district lines and how childhood poverty is being confronted.

Most directly it will require us to reimagine the content presented in the classroom, *how* it's presented, and *who* presents it to better foster students' empathy for people different from themselves. Transforming education through empathy inspires a deeper understanding of other perspectives, increases students' awareness of privilege, and reminds them of the shared moral imperative to improve the world for others, rather than oneself alone.

Part of this transformation will require us to bring conversations about difficult topics into a child's personal and academic development at an earlier stage, but many teachers and parents are hesitant to approach these subjects because of the sensitivities—and sometimes traumas—involved.

One thing that is clear, however, is that trying to shield children from these topics is unlikely to work either. Multiple studies suggest that children become aware of racial differences from a surprisingly young age. Research has shown that nine-month-old infants use race to categorize faces, three-year-old children associate certain racial groups with negative traits, and by age four, children in many nations associate White people with wealth and higher social status.[3]

Children can unknowingly bring these biases into the classroom, and they can take a lifetime to unlearn if not addressed at a formative age. Teachers are on the front lines of getting this right, but they themselves can fall prey to their own biases and misunderstandings, even when motivated by the best intentions.

For example, many classrooms around the world fail to teach children history or literature from a perspective beyond that of the conquering European nations which colonized regions across the globe (including America). Perhaps the most ubiquitous yet overlooked symbol of this is the standard map of the Earth used in classrooms all over the world.

For generations, worldwide classrooms have used the Mercator projection map despite the fact that it grossly misrepresents the relative sizes of the continents and places North America and Europe literally in the center of the world. More accurate world maps have emerged in recent years, and several professional geographic societies have even recommended a ban on the outdated Mercator maps.

Despite these criticisms, the centuries-old Mercator projection continues to be the most widely printed and used format—even in regions that its design inherently discriminates against such as Africa and Asia.

The **True Size** of **Africa**

A small contribution in the fight against rampant *Immappancy,* by **Kai Krause**

United States   Europe   India

Japan   China

(cc) **creative commons**

Examples like this remind us of the importance of questioning long-standing bias in the lessons we teach, whether they're built into the curriculum teachers use or plainly visible in the maps hanging on classroom walls.

Thankfully, plenty of educators and students alike are starting to ask these kinds of questions, and they are demanding meaningful change both in and outside of the classroom.

How Things Are Changing . . .

When Kaleena Sales, a professor of graphic design at Tennessee State University and one of this book's contributors, recounts her time working as a designer in the predominantly White advertising industry, she describes a dynamic where her work repeatedly "needed to blend into White-dominant culture to be deemed legitimate."

In the field of design education, decades of programs have prioritized the study and appreciation of European design and treated other cultures as secondary or ignored them altogether. It is a bias Sales has taken strides to correct in her teaching by intentionally showcasing the work of more diverse artists and helping her students to discover their own unique styles.

"Too often [young Black designers'] portfolios must communicate an appreciation for European design and only showcase Black and urban design in specific brand choices. Even more troubling is that we sometimes fail to recognize it as a problem."

Kaleena Sales, Professor and Author

Shifts in education regularly start like this, with one dedicated teacher deciding to introduce students to a broader perspective. They can also begin with how openly and honestly we choose to talk to children about difficult topics outside of school.

As a Black father of six, this was a choice Jelani Memory faced while raising his multicultural family. Racism was an unavoidable topic of conversation. In his journey to find ways of approaching the subject with his young kids, he decided to publish a book with an unusually serious title: *A Kids Book About Racism*. In it he offers a simplified and engaging description of what racism is, how it makes people feel when they experience it, and how to spot it when it happens.

After parents, teachers and caregivers all responded positively to the book's format and candor, Memory went on to launch A Kids Book About—a children's book publishing company that now includes titles on empathy, feminism, White privilege, belonging, gender, immigration, autism, and more, all written by a wide range of diverse authors. Outside of schools and curricula, the stories that we share with children through media and entertainment are also important tools to help them imagine a more diverse and inclusive world.

This mission also describes the work of master puppeteer Marilyn Price. For decades she has used her puppets to tell global stories and show children that despite our differences, there are even more things we all have in common.

"I greet a variety of not just cultures, but learners. And puppets work for that. Kids get it, and often they are the ones to teach it to their parents."

Marilyn Price, Master Puppeteer

Whether through books, TV, or live puppet shows, there is a growing appetite for diverse learning materials at all age levels. Over time this diversity may eventually become part of the "traditional" curriculum, as it has already in New Zealand.

When asked about what makes the system of schooling in his country unique, New Zealand elementary school principal Clifford Wicks says, "We recognize the benefits that are gained for all students from learning the indigenous language of the country of their birth or residency. The concept of unity through diversity is embedded within the school culture."[4]

Students in New Zealand learn basic te reo, the indigenous Māori language, and they are taught to respectfully perform the Māori war dance known as the *haka*.

The story of diversity within education is evolving unevenly across the globe. There are regional pockets (like New Zealand) where this has become a priority, and there are places where the opposite still holds true. Until there is more equity across regions, districts, and nations, this mission to achieve a more diverse educational system will remain incomplete.

To shift more of the world's regions toward this reality, let's take a look at where institutions must focus their energies and resources.

What Needs To Happen...

The push for our modern educational system to better prepare our youth for a more inclusive world must become an urgent priority. Higher education, in particular, is starting to feel this urgency. The industry is facing increased scrutiny, not only over the escalating cost of a four-year degree, but also because its curriculum has too often proven incomplete in preparing students for life in the real world.

This criticism of a lack of real-world relevance is leveled at elementary and high school programs as well. To address this issue, educational institutions for students of all ages must work harder to integrate lessons on topics such as racial literacy and cultural inclusion into school curricula. What can we do as citizens, parents, students, and educators to help accelerate this process?

We suggest starting with the following priorities.

IMPERATIVE #1

Educational institutions must address inequity and racism in and out of the classroom.

In the book *Diversity at College,* a group of recent graduates share their personal struggles as students, all while offering an actionable roadmap for students, faculty, and administrators for genuine learning about diversity in higher education. The book imagines a future where these types of conversations are commonplace within the educational system, and where students from different backgrounds are all equally encouraged and supported as individuals.

The starting point must be an educational system that is willing to reframe sometimes intimidating conversations about race, justice, diversity, and equity as an opportunity for growth and learning, rather than a breeding ground for conflict and blame. One initiative working to make this a reality is the Anti-Racist Teaching and Learning Collective (ARTLC), which was built as a network for educators seeking to diversify and expand their curriculum. The program has already helped teachers to adjust history lessons to center Indigenous peoples and teach international relations from a colonized group's perspective.

——— IMPERATIVE #2 ———

Diversifying the teaching workforce must become a priority at every age level of education.

The value of educators from varied backgrounds cannot be overstated. Research shows that teachers of color are more likely to have higher expectations for students of color (as measured by higher numbers of referrals to gifted programs); they are more likely to confront issues of racism head-on; and they're more likely to develop trusting relationships with other students, particularly those with whom they share a cultural background.

Unfortunately, the teaching profession has long suffered from a demographic imbalance. In the US alone, the National Center for Education Statistics found that 79 percent of all public-school teachers identify as White—a percentage that has seen little fluctuation in the last 15 years.[5] Meanwhile, according to the Public School Review, more than half of students aged pre-K to eighth grade in the US are from a minority group.[6]

Among educators, this same homogeneity applies to other axes of identity as well, like gender and education level: 77 percent of teachers are female, and almost 50 percent have a master's degree.[7] When student diversity isn't mirrored in school faculty and staff, it can create inequitable power dynamics and send the harmful message that teaching is only meant for certain groups of people.

What does it look like to support educator diversity? For starters, recruitment and hiring departments should minimize the financial barriers that pursuing a teaching career poses, namely, the several advanced degrees unnecessarily listed as a prerequisite. Instead, hiring teachers who come through alternative certification programs or who have foreign teaching backgrounds can broaden the hiring pool and bring more non-traditional yet equally qualified perspectives to the classroom.

IMPERATIVE #3

Support student-led initiatives, demands, and ideas to foster or promote diversity at school.

One lesson we share often in this book is that it is critical to *always listen* directly to the people you're trying to advocate for—in this case, students and teachers.

Today, many forward-thinking students are holding their institutions accountable by calling for structural changes that would have an immediate impact on the equity and inclusiveness of their entire campus experience.

Within the classroom, students are demanding core curriculum to be overhauled and replaced with a more globally-minded and social justice-focused perspective. Some schools have listened to their feedback and revised required reading lists and mandatory classes, filtering them through a diversity lens.

Other structural changes can be more culture-oriented than curricular. For years, colleges have offered affinity groups for students of color to gather, hold dialogue together, and share their experiences. Now, more and more high schools are following suit, introducing the values of identity-based community earlier on in a student's academic development. Groups have also been created for those in social majorities who want to consider how they can support and uplift students of other identities. The more we can encourage this kind of student-led organizing, the better.

What You Can Do . . .

Today, the demand is clear: students want, need, and deserve an education built on the principles of inclusion and equity. In a world that constantly oscillates between moments of encouraging connectedness and disappointing division, learning about diversity, equity and inclusion has already emerged as a key competency for people hoping to be successful students and, later on, successful leaders and members of society.

To add your voice to the movement, consider these action steps.

Seek out, buy, and consume more diverse children's educational content.

We need to be curious about the content our children consume. The stories which surround them are the stories that help them to grow, informing their childhoods through imagination. Stories give us knowledge, resilience and compassion. But who is invisible, absent or underrepresented in these narratives? And is each characters' portrayal truly authentic?

Every culture's history is essential. Everyone deserves to have their lives elevated through the beauty of truthful representation. But what message are we sending to children who don't see themselves in their favorite shows?'

These are the kinds of questions you can ask as a de facto curator of educational materials, whether you are a parent, aunt, grandparent, or even an older sibling. Cerrie Burnell, an author and Disability Ambassador for the BBC, offers this advice: "If you're a parent, read as diversely as you can to your children and let them lead the way as well—because reading has value."

 Download our diverse reading list for kids at www.nonobviousdiversity.com/resources

The most important reminder is to do your homework to ensure that the diverse stories being told are authentic ones, not superficial portrayals. Becky Curran Kekula, the disability equality index director at Disability:IN, describes herself as a little person who proudly identifies as part of the disability community. In her experience, the impact of diverse storytelling as it relates to children's education can be life altering.

"The reason why authentic storytelling is so important to me is that historically people with dwarfism have been portrayed as leprechauns or elves, and then people in society think we are those characters in real life."

Becky Curran Kekula, Disability Advocate

When kids see little people as complex humans with real lives rather than stereotypical characters, it breaks down a lot of the ableist stigma that kids unintentionally inherit from the mainstream media.

ACTION #2

Get involved locally and start your own diversity initiative.

When it comes to DEI, many think grand gestures are necessary for impact. But education is all around us, and sometimes it's better to think and act small and scale up from there. When Chhavi Arya, one of the contributors to this book, discovered a lack of curricula teaching elementary school kids about multiculturalism in her Greater Essex County school district in Canada, she created her own.

"Books, worksheets, and every lesson plan should reflect the diversity of our world and the identities of all students. It's up to educators to bring diverse and inclusive storytellers, food, music, art, clothing, language and sports etc. into the classroom and incorporate them into the subjects they teach. When you start small and encourage students to think differently, you create an experience that can equip them with knowledge and a perspective they will use for the rest of their life."

Chhavi Arya, Co-Founder of Ideapress Publishing and Former Public School Teacher

Several years later, her on-the-ground efforts inspired educators to implement a broader curriculum across all of Ontario. Nearly two decades later, Chhavi produced and co-hosted our Non-Obvious Beyond Diversity Summit alongside Rohit and Jennifer. Whether you are a teacher, a parent, or simply a concerned citizen, your own involvement can start small. You never know what your efforts will spark within your community—or your own life.

Hold the institutions you are part of accountable for identifying and fixing inequity.

Now more than ever, young adults are stepping into their power as agents of change in their local communities. For example, in 2019 students at Georgetown University voted to pay a tax of $27.20 per student per semester to create a fund that would pay reparations to descendants of hundreds of enslaved people sold by the university in 1838. In early 2021, students at Brown University also voted for their school to offer reparations to descendants of enslaved people affiliated with their institution.

This type of advocacy and autonomy is within your control. Challenge yourself to point out the stereotypes you see in movies, television, video games, books—all the content we are constantly surrounded with. By doing this or identifying exclusion when you see it, you normalize these discussions and make them easier to have. In time, this will allow conversations about identity and inclusion to deepen as we all grow.

As the students from the stories above illustrate, you don't need to wait for administrators to make the first move. You can decide to do something on your own. The belief at the heart of movements like these is that we need to demand more of our leadership— more transparency, more action, more accountability. By staying critical and fighting for the type of education you believe in, you can push educational leaders to do and be better.

Beyond Diversity In
EDUCATION

🏛 WHAT NEEDS TO HAPPEN:

- ❯ Educational institutions must address inequity and racism in and out of the classroom.
- ❯ Diversifying the teaching workforce must become a priority at every age level of education.
- ❯ Support student-led initiatives, demands, and ideas to foster or promote diversity at school.

WHAT *YOU* CAN DO:

- ❯ Seek out, buy, and consume more diverse children's educational content.
- ❯ Get involved locally and start your own diversity initiative.
- ❯ Hold the institutions you are part of accountable for identifying and fixing inequity.

💬 CONVERSATION STARTERS:

- ❯ Looking back on your upbringing, what perspectives were missing?
- ❯ What was a formative moment in your education that shifted your perspective of yourself, others, or the world?
- ❯ How many teachers did you have in elementary school who were BIPOC or disabled?

BEYOND DIVERSITY IN
RETAIL

"Diversity and inclusion, which are the real grounds for creativity, must remain at the center of what we do."

— *Marco Bizzarri, CEO of Gucci*

Chapter Summary:

The retail sector has often sold one-dimensional products or offered store experiences that can exclude BIPOC, LGBTQ+ and disabled consumers. Recent efforts to eliminate bias in advertising, make product design more inclusive, buy from diverse suppliers and make hiring more equitable are helping retailers appeal to consumers who are increasingly demanding these inclusive practices.

How It Is . . .

Fashion is one of the most basic forms of self-expression. The way we dress makes a statement about how we'd like to be seen by others and how we see ourselves. But for nonbinary or gender diverse people, finding clothes that are gender non-specific can be a stressful experience in a highly-gendered world.

In 2018, former fashion executive Rob Smith decided to do something about this crucial gap in retail. After quitting his corporate job, Rob founded the Phluid Project in Manhattan, one of the world's first gender-neutral retail stores.

As a gay man, Rob recalls feeling pressured to make painful choices about how he presented himself to the world. As a young boy he felt pressured to play sports instead of playing with dolls, and later on, as a corporate executive, he was constantly told he needed to dress a certain way if he wanted to succeed. He founded the Phluid Project as a healing decision to offer the safe, expressive space his younger self never had.

His idea resonated with many other people, and it quickly evolved into more than just a clothing store. Rob and his team created a global online community for those who believe in gender-neutral fashion. The Phluid Project now serves as a safe place for transgender, gender-diverse, and queer people, and as a hub where community events and casual hangouts are hosted.

Eventually Rob hopes to establish a career networking program for community members to connect with open-minded, inclusive retail companies looking to hire diverse employees.

Unfortunately, most retail environments aren't as inclusive as the Phluid Project. Whether it's apparel retailers, grocery stores, restaurants, beauty salons, or even online shopping platforms, the world of retail commerce is by and large designed for consumers of specific backgrounds or body types. For those who fall outside the accepted parameters, shopping can be an excluding or even hostile experience.

More than 60 percent of Black Americans say they have experienced racial discrimination inside a retail store— an experience so widely shared that it is commonly described among those who have encountered it as "shopping while Black" and refers to everything from being followed around a store to being ignored or skipped over in favor of non-Black customers.[1]

79% of retail shoppers struggle to find associates who look like them.

SOURCE: The Racial Bias In Retail Report 2021

In early 2021, retailer Sephora commissioned a study to examine the scope of racial bias in retail.[2] The majority of BIPOC US retail shoppers who participated in the study believed skin color and ethnicity were the primary lenses through which sales associates judged them.

Fair treatment in retail is not only an issue for nonbinary, gender nonconforming, or BIPOC consumers either. Nearly three-quarters of disabled customers say they feel forced to shop online due to limited accessibility at physical stores.[3] Plus-size clothing shoppers also regularly report what Kathryn H. Anthony, architecture professor and author of *Designing for Diversity*, calls "the plus-size displacement," where everything from the size of fitting rooms to the back-of-the-store placement of plus-sized clothing communicates bias against those with larger bodies.[4]

75% percent of disabled customers had to leave a store or website because they could not finish a purchase due to their disability.

Source: Purple UK

Stereotypes also persist in the design of products sold in retail. Many disabled parents, for example, regularly have trouble finding bassinets or strollers that can attach to a wheelchair.

Other studies show that the design of virtual-reality headsets is more likely to give women motion sickness, because 90 percent of women have pupils closer together than the typical headset's default *male* setting.[5] In each case, the needs of one group are prioritized while the needs of another are almost completely ignored.

Ironically, the retail economy also has a habit of excluding the one group of consumers who have the *most* money to spend: seniors.

The spending power of this "silver economy," composed of people over the age of 60, surpassed $15 trillion in 2020.

Despite this literal wealth of potential, general media still depicts older people in stereotypical ways most of the time, if they are even depicted at all. The advertising industry is even worse, particularly in America where ads have a history of ignoring older consumers in nearly every sector except the manipulative "ask your doctor if [insert drug name] is right for you" pharmaceutical ads.

If the products we buy and the services we use (as well as the advertising that promotes them) became more inclusive, the entire retail landscape could follow suit. It would not only affect *what* we buy and consume but also *where* we buy it and *who* is involved in the design, production, and distribution of making and selling it.

"Inclusive teams that value diverse perspectives and inclusive design principles will have the deepest impact in building products designed for everyone."

Satya Nadella, CEO of Microsoft

Fixing the broken aspects of retail will require a multi-faceted response because it spans so many business silos, from store layout and product development to advertising strategies and package designs. The lens of diversity and inclusion needs to be applied widely to each of these elements, and big questions need to be asked and answered.

Are products designed by a representative team? Are they advertised with an inclusive cast of actors and models of all ages? Is the selling environment of those products or services inclusive and accessible? Many retailers have already started finding solutions to these questions. Let's look at some examples.

How Things Are Changing . . .

To examine how diversity and inclusivity might look in retail, an obvious place to start would be with food. Many restaurants and grocery stores have been started, staffed, and supported by a wide diversity of non-White, often immigrant entrepreneurs. Small neighborhood grocery stores, in particular, provide access for culturally diverse families to buy familiar products that may be unavailable at larger retailers. They also serve as distribution points for media and entertainment unavailable elsewhere. For example, almost every Indian immigrant family, as Rohit fondly recalls, grew up renting Bollywood movies on VHS (and eventually on DVD) from their local Indian grocery store.

Local immigrant-run grocery stores and restaurants often serve as cultural ambassadors who can confront stereotypes and demystify what might otherwise seem like different and unapproachable cultures. Restaurants have long offered a gateway for local communities to explore the food and traditions of the rest of the world without leaving home.

Beyond showcasing other cultures, some of the most forward-looking retail experiences involve grocery retailers focusing on a different type of inclusion—for neurodiverse individuals. For example, Australian grocery retailer Coles partnered with Autism Spectrum Australia (Aspect) to create a "sensory-friendly experience" by going quiet for an hour. They limited announcements, reduced customers, and dimmed the lights in order to help improve the shopping experience of people and families with members on the autism spectrum.[6]

This idea of sensory-friendly experiences is now extending to all types of retailers. In the past year alone, we encountered stories of barbershops, restaurants, airport stores, and even destinations like zoos and sports stadiums experimenting with creating environments that are more welcoming and accessible for all kinds of people.

Taking this same concept beyond the store experience, retailers also have the unique opportunity to build a more inclusive world by directly supporting and buying from businesses owned by underrepresented entrepreneurs. Big-box retailer Target has been particularly aggressive in this arena, and they have publicly committed to spending more than $2 billion with Black-owned businesses by 2025.[7]

On an industry-wide level, the 15 Percent Pledge is a US-based nonprofit organization that encourages retailers to pledge at least 15 percent of their shelf space to Black-owned businesses. The movement was established in 2020 by Aurora James, and Sephora was the first large retailer to sign onto the pledge and use its merchandising prowess to turn shopping into activism. In the short time since, several other companies have joined, including Gap, Banana Republic, Crate and Barrel, and Macy's, to name a few.

Another important factor driving inclusivity in retail is the creation of product categories that didn't even exist a decade ago. In beauty and fashion, for example, more brands are investing in lines of makeup for men. Barbie, long known for their iconic dolls for girls, started marketing to children of all genders. LEGO launched their somewhat controversial but still wildly successful LEGO Friends line based on deep research into the variations in how different groups of children like to play.[8] Ballet Black, a UK-based ballet company that has promoted dancers of Black and Asian descent for more than two decades, partnered with shoemaker Freed in 2019 to create pointe (ballet) shoes to match a variety of darker skin tones. A company called Reframd sells eyeglasses designed with wider nose bridges for the facial profiles of Black people. Online retailer Zappos even has a program where they sell single shoes for amputees.

Some retailers are even finding success in taking the *same* product they have always sold and promoting it to entire segments of consumers they had previously ignored. For decades, most motorcycle brands focused solely on selling bikes to men. Recently, Harley-Davidson, Ducati, and Triumph have all built robust divisions selling motorcycles to women, and the fastest-growing demographic of motorcycle buyers is women, who now represent up to one in five riders—nearly double the numbers from a decade ago.[9]

These examples illustrate the rapid evolution happening in the world of retail, and this pace is on track to continue for the foreseeable future.

What Needs To Happen...

To see a world where both the "IRL" (in real life) and "URL" (online) marketplaces are tailored for all types of customers, both sellers and buyers will need to make more intentional decisions and put their money where their mouth is.

Using the rich advice gleaned from the Non-Obvious Beyond Diversity Summit and all its speakers, we identified several key areas for retailers to focus on in the near future.

IMPERATIVE #1

Teams designing products and crafting in-store experiences must cater to a broader customer identity base.

The journey to diversifying product lineups always starts in retail by responding to a consumer need. Often, it is a consumer who has previously felt ignored or marginalized. Uncovering the opportunity, however, requires both a willingness to listen to what consumers are saying, and prioritizing making product development teams more inclusive so these new perspectives can be championed from inside the organization by someone who has lived that same experience.

For example, Nike took input from athletes, advocates, and employees to develop a hijab for Muslim athletes that performed well and met cultural requirements.[10]

By creating the Pro Hijab, Nike sends an important message about inclusion and encourages a generation of Muslim girls to think of themselves as athletes. Recognizing its significance, *Time* magazine named it one of the best inventions of the year in 2017.

This push for more inclusive products has become more widespread in the years since then. Tommy Hilfiger launched an "Adaptive Fashion" line for disabled consumers that featured open necklines, extended zipper pulls, magnetic buttons, wide leg openings, and sliding drawcords. Adidas has introduced a new line of "burkinis" not only for veiled women, but also for those who may be more sensitive to the sun.

"Industries need to be shamed and they need to understand that disabled people have the buying power of the entire country of China. Eight trillion dollars. People don't think of us as viewers. They don't think of us as buyers. They don't think of us as an audience."

Maysoon Zayid, Comedian and Disability Advocate

In addition to product design, the retail environment itself must become more inclusive as well. Thanks to the efforts of several American retailers—including Target, Wegmans, and Walgreens—and destinations such as the Smithsonian National Zoo, blind and low-vision individuals now have access to wearable technology, artificial intelligence, and even live human assistance through technology from San Diego-based startup Aira that offers real-time visual descriptions to customers through streaming video.

These efforts to make in-person experiences more welcoming for all not only engage more people and improve satisfaction scores, they typically lead to increased revenue as well.

—— IMPERATIVE #2 ——

Marketers must trade tokenism in advertising for authentic representation.

By developing ads that reflect diverse people's everyday experiences, retailers can establish an authentic connection with shoppers. The inclusion of LGBTQ+ people in advertising is a good example of this.

There was a time when showing a gay couple in an ad would cause angry backlash from conservative groups, and advertisers would be forced to pull such ads off the air. Today, the backlash comes if the ad *does* get pulled. According to a recent story from

CNN, so many brands have chosen to feature gay couples that it has become a "mainstream phenomenon."[11]

Simply including diverse people in advertising doesn't always mean they are depicted in inclusive ways, however. Savvy consumers can detect when organizations are merely attempting to fill a diversity quota without communicating the deeper message in an authentic, believable way.

75% of Gen Z consumers would end relationships with companies that run advertising campaigns perceived as sexist, racist, or homophobic.

Source: McKinsey

On this note, brands must be careful to avoid exoticizing their "diverse" models or actors. Vimbayi Kajese is the founder of #Adtags, a proudly African-based marketplace that helps conscious brands source images featuring people of color for their advertising campaigns. She says retailers can often "other" or objectify their models of color, which negatively impacts the customers the brand is trying to reach. Brands need to be intentional and respectful about the images they create, and ask themselves, are we doing this because it feels authentic and meaningful . . . or because we are simply just trying to check a box labeled "inclusive"?

 Download our guide to inclusive imagery at www.nonobviousdiversity.com/resources

Organizations must go beyond "feel-good metrics" and match actions to words.

Once an organization signals a commitment to diversity, deciding which metrics to prioritize is key in ensuring these commitments are substantive rather than performative. Measuring the diversity of an employee workforce, for example, seems like a positive metric on the surface. Yet if a company has a 75 percent "diverse" workforce, but that diversity only exists among low-paid roles for hourly floor workers, a better metric to focus on would be the percentage of people on the *leadership* team who come from underrepresented groups.

When a leadership team is diverse, not only can they imagine and prioritize creating a retail experience that is more inclusive, but they can also help spot potential issues or controversies that might be invisible to leaders who lack the same perspective.

What You Can Do . . .

The importance and economic power of diversity in retail will only increase with time. Generations like millennials (those born 1981 to 1996) and Gen Z (those born 1997 to 2015) actively value equity and make critical buying decisions based on it.

One study found that 65 percent of consumers aged 18–34 said they would shop more at a retailer that offers a wider selection of multicultural products.[12] The study also found that 47 percent of that same age group would pay more for a brand that really understands their multicultural needs.

Some of the required changes are systemic, but we all have buying power as consumers and advocacy power as employees. Let's look at three steps we can all take to support greater equity and diversity in retail.

——————— **ACTION #1** ———————

When you see bias in retail, call it out and demand for it to change.

———————————————————————

There are many ways that retail experiences can feel hostile to those customer identities who've been neglected. Many of them are not the product of intentional bias, but are rather due to ignorance or maintaining a longstanding status quo.

Examples include stock images that depict only people of a certain skin tone or body type. Items designed for more diverse consumers could be buried at the back of the store. Store aisles might make it impossible for someone in a wheelchair to navigate, or place products too high and out of reach. Hair and beauty products for women of color might be kept in locked displays while products for other ethnicities sit openly on the shelves. These are examples of retail injustices, and they can persist if no one calls them out.

Approach every retail experience with more awareness of these biases and choose not to ignore them by voicing your concerns. Retailers react to consumer complaints—particularly if they hear the same concern from multiple people. When you see something, say something.

If not for yourself, then do it for those other consumers who could benefit from your speaking on their behalf.

—————— **ACTION #2** ——————

Wield your consumer power responsibly by doing your homework.

Johanna Zeilstra is the CEO of Gender Fair, an independent platform that makes it easy for consumers to shop their values. The Gender Fair app rates companies on various diversity-based criteria and offers real-time ratings of more than 800 companies, representing 2,500 brands to help consumers make purchasing decisions at all points of sale. Johanna says that supporting purpose-driven and mission-oriented brands may be the strongest tool at the customer's disposal.

Capitalism itself can be a form of advocacy if we are willing to reward those brands in the marketplace through our consumer power. There are more organizations creating tools and services like Gender Fair's app to make it easy to be informed by simply scanning a logo, label or barcode with a smartphone.

Research suggests that this is going to be more and more important as time goes on. For example, one study found that brands who display a broad variety of cultural and demographic groups in advertising garnered an average stock gain of 44 percent in a seven-quarter period, and brands with the highest diversity scores from a comprehensive audit showed an 83 percent higher consumer preference.

It may be tempting to see the effects of your individual purchasing decisions as insignificant, but the accumulation of these choices can equate to big changes—and it does indeed start with you.

ACTION #3

Buy from more diverse suppliers for yourself and on behalf of organizations.

Every purchase you make is a chance for you to support more diversity in retail. Are you indiscriminately buying everything you need from Amazon, or will you support local businesses like independent bookstores, even if it means paying an extra dollar or two?

Most of us have moments when we have a chance to spend other people's money as well. Perhaps you are buying jerseys for a soccer team or choosing a caterer for your next family reunion. There are many examples of moments when you can act on an individual level the same way a supplier or diversity manager might act on behalf of an organization.

And if you are working in an organization that doesn't have someone in charge of selecting suppliers, you can start a supplier diversity program yourself to source your materials and products from new, more diverse vendors.

All of these represent choices *you* can make to use funds at your disposal—whether they're personal or belong to an organization you're a part of—to encourage more diversity in retail and to support it where it already exists.

Beyond Diversity In
RETAIL

🏛 WHAT NEEDS TO HAPPEN:

- Teams designing products and in-store experiences must cater to a broader customer identity base.
- Marketers must trade tokenism in advertising for authentic representation.
- Organizations must go beyond "feel-good metrics" and match actions to words.

👆 WHAT *YOU* CAN DO:

- When you see bias in retail, call it out and demand for it to change.
- Wield your consumer power responsibly by doing your homework.
- Buy from more diverse suppliers for yourself and on behalf of other organizations.

💬 CONVERSATION STARTERS:

- What are the values most important to you and which specific retailers share those priorities?
- Can you identify 2-3 ways that a retail store's layout or placement of products may be biased and proactively raise these concerns with a store owner/manager?

7

BEYOND DIVERSITY IN
THE WORKPLACE

"In the past jobs were about muscles,
now they're about brains, but in the
future they'll be about the heart."

— *Dame Nemat Shafik, Director of
the London School of Economics*

Chapter Summary:

*Many people from underrepresented groups feel pressure
to assimilate into a dominant workplace culture and
are reluctant to be themselves at work. Hiring practices
can also regularly exclude candidates from marginalized
backgrounds. Creating a more inclusive workplace requires
DEI training, fundamental shifts in hiring processes, and fair
and equitable opportunities for career advancement.*

How It Is . . .

As a child, Dr. Dave Caudel says he fantasized about a UFO landing on Earth and coming to his school. He would imagine the aliens approaching him and saying, "There's been a huge mistake, and we're here to take you home."[1]

Feeling like he was from a different planet is an analogy Caudel uses to explain how little the world around him seemed to understand how he communicated. As an adult, he was diagnosed with Asperger syndrome, a developmental condition affecting one's ability to effectively socialize. Learning to turn his condition into an asset has been a lifelong journey.

Today Caudel is the executive director of the Frist Center for Autism and Innovation at Vanderbilt University, where he and his team bring together engineers and researchers in order to understand the potential for neurodiverse talent in the modern workplace—and foster strengths-based conversations about how neurodiverse workers such as those with autism can excel in certain roles.

Sam Latif is legally blind and works as a special consultant for inclusive design at Procter & Gamble (P&G). For more than a decade, she has worked to find new ways of making P&G products more accessible. In 2018, she spearheaded a push to add raised dashes or dots to Herbal Essences hair-care products so people with low vision could tell the difference between bottles of shampoo and conditioner solely through touch.

Both Latif and Caudel illustrate the benefits of building more diverse workplaces. While this might seem like a recent revelation, when it comes to building neurodiverse teams or hiring employees with disabilities, the truth is that an inclusive workplace has long been a key element in delivering more user-friendly products and services.

When people of some genders, races, abilities, ethnicities, religions and more are excluded from the workplace, the products and services delivered (not to mention the ads that promote them) miss out on appealing to a wider market, and sometimes even lead to major backlash.

For years, Crayola labeled its peach-colored crayon "flesh," which provided a constant reminder to children of color that their skin was not viewed as "the norm" in society. Band-Aid only produced bandages in one color—meant to match the skin of White people—until very recently. Fashion brands to this day continue to promote shoes and pantyhose in one "nude" color, which only matches lighter skin tones.

97% of HR managers say employees with disabilities perform the same or better than peers without disabilities.

Source: Society for Human Resource Management (SHRM)

These are the kinds of products we've come to expect from homogenous teams working in places that either lack diversity or fail to listen to the marginalized voices on their team. Changing this reality requires recruiting and hiring more diverse team members, and ensuring that their unique perspectives are not silenced, but respected and acted upon.

The truth is, regardless of whether someone comes from a neurodiverse background, has a physical disability, or belongs to an underrepresented gender, ethnicity, or age group, most marginalized people describe feeling pressure at some point in their careers to assimilate into a dominant culture. As a result, many are denied the chance to truly flourish in their chosen field.

"Ultimately, we need to work our way out of the consulting business. While that is how our work in the industry was born, we want to be a conduit to getting Muslim writers to be the ones creating stories instead of just advising on them."

Sue Obeidi, Muslim Public Affairs Council

This entire cycle starts with the difficulty that many of these professionals experience during the hiring process itself. Biased language in job descriptions can discourage women and diverse candidates from applying. Hiring teams themselves often lack diversity and personal biases can lead to homogeneous candidate pools.

And if they *are* hired, many underrepresented employees lack role models in senior positions who look like them or can serve as mentors or sponsors and provide pathways to leadership roles for high potential talent. Each of these challenges illustrates just how stacked the odds can be against some workers and their aspirations.

Ageism is also a growing issue in the workplace. The contributions of older workers in our culture are frequently minimized. As the average age of workers increases, people want and need to be productive longer. Unfortunately, policies such as mandatory retirement ages and a continuing recruitment bias against hiring older workers can create a difficult situation for those over age 55.

"Older workers are underappreciated, and older consumers are often ignored. While people over 50 today are healthier, more educated, working and living longer . . . age discrimination remains more prevalent than ever."

Andrea Roane, Retired News Anchor and Reporter, WUSA9 (CBS)

The solutions to many of these issues need to include understanding how bias impacts decisions, creating goals for increasing diversity in the workforce and holding people accountable for their part in achieving those goals. In addition, organizations must rethink recruiting processes, ensure equitable opportunities, and in some cases, even redesign the physical environment of the workplace.

To see how this might happen in practice, let's review some examples of organizations that have already started.

How Things Are Changing . . .

José Velasco is the chief program manager of product engineering at SAP, a multinational software corporation. He is also an ambassador for the SAP Autism at Work program, an initiative focused on hiring employees on the autism spectrum.

The program launched in 2013 and was one of the first of its kind to intentionally focus on the hiring of neurodiverse candidates. The program helps SAP tap into an underutilized talent pool—and it starts with the hiring process itself.

15% of the world's population have some form of disability.

Source: World Health Organization

As Velasco described during our summit, SAP has implemented several innovative choices to make the recruiting journey fairer for those who might otherwise struggle during a traditional hiring process.

Here's an example: candidates are given interview questions beforehand and told that eye contact is optional. The ultimate goal is to remove factors that can cause anxiety for neurodiverse candidates (such as on-the-spot questioning) and allow them to really showcase talents that might otherwise be overshadowed in a traditional interviewing process. The program has inspired many similar initiatives in the tech industry, and boasts an impressive 90 percent retention rate.

Other companies have taken a different approach. Ultranauts Inc. founded in 2013 by two MIT engineers, aims to create a "universal workplace" where cognitively diverse teams can thrive. Seventy-five percent of the company's team members are on the autism spectrum. Co-founder and CEO Rajesh Anandan notes that "when you bring together different brain types, you can solve more complex problems. But in order to truly benefit from a cognitively diverse team, you need to do more than offer accommodations."

Inclusive hiring programs have shown promising results for decades outside the technology industry as well. Back in 1970, less than 20 percent of musicians in major symphony orchestras were women. To make auditions more equitable, symphony directors experimented with anonymous auditions by hanging a screen between a musician and the evaluators, in order to judge musicians on their sound alone. Over the next 20 years, the number of women hired by major symphony orchestras more than doubled.

This widely shared story is spotlighted in the book *Blind Spot* by psychology professors Mahzarin R. Banaji and Anthony G. Greenwald as an example of how long-standing bias can be isolated and conquered.

Fast forwarding to modern times, in 2021 the European Space Agency specifically sought out people with disabilities as potential astronauts so they could better study what adaptations to space stations might be necessary to accommodate them.[2] In 2018,

Starbucks opened its first "Signing Store" for the deaf and hard of hearing just a few blocks from the internationally renowned Gallaudet University. More than 75 percent of baristas at the location have a hearing disability and all are proficient in American Sign Language.[3]

Inclusive teams have become a priority in many governments as well. At the US Department of Homeland Security (DHS), Assistant Director Scott Lanum explains, "There's no possibility of getting it right if we don't have an organization that is composed of people who come from different backgrounds." For Lanum, the number one recruiting priority is bringing more female law enforcement officers into the immigration enforcement workforce.

To make this a reality, DHS holds quarterly meetings to discuss hiring pipelines and runs a mentorship program for women in law enforcement. There have already been signs of progress. Approximately 47 percent of the DHS workforce identify as people of color, and women now comprise about 36 percent of the DHS future leadership pool.

Despite initiatives like these across many public and private organizations, however, the goal of a fully diverse and inclusive workplace remains an elusive one for many organizations. In order to get closer to this vision, some key priorities need to be set.

What Needs To Happen . . .

Right now, stories of inclusive hiring and training programs are celebrated because they are relatively rare. Over time these programs will ideally become less unusual and more commonplace.

An inclusive hiring program should be the default.

How can we shape a world where workplaces are more inclusive and welcoming to those who present themselves outside the usual employee blueprint? Here are three ideas to start with.

IMPERATIVE #1

Leaders must recognize that great diversity exists within marginalized groups.

When we seek to add new members to our teams, we must remember that this could mean diversity of gender, nationality, race, or experience, and even within these dimensions there are significant differences. For example, according to the Pew Research Center, 23 million Asian Americans trace their roots to more than 46 countries in East and Southeast Asia and the Indian subcontinent, each with unique histories, cultures, and languages. When we talk about disability, we need to recognize that significant diversity exists within that category as well: there are cognitive disabilities, physical or mobility-based disabilities, and sensory-related disabilities.

Focusing on building a more diverse team by hiring a single individual who is "diverse" can quickly become tokenism. Diversity at work must not be reduced to checking boxes or filling quotas. Hiring the first woman, person of color, disabled person, formerly incarcerated person, or person from any other marginalized group doesn't mean the job is finished.

"The best teams I've been on have been more like a family than a team, because I know I can pick up the phone and those people are going to be there for me if I need them. This is true whether you look at the military or across any other space."

Lt Colonel Jennifer "JJ" Snow, Air Force/AFWERX
Chief Technology Officer

The reason diversity quotas or affirmative action initiatives exist is to open a door that might otherwise be shut. But opening that door just enough to let one person through and then letting it shut once more isn't the progress we need. Nor is hiring from diverse talent pools, but then not providing equitable opportunities for those same hires to progress in their careers.

Building a truly equitable and inclusive workforce where people can treat one another like family means gathering people of different skills, points of view, and backgrounds together— and then building an environment where every perspective is respected and included, and where all employees are treated fairly.

Organizations need to listen to what people need and ensure those needs are met.

Beyond bringing in a more diverse pool of people, organizations also need to create inclusive work environments where they can succeed. For some employees, this may mean accommodations such as reserved parking, flexible work arrangements, or making documentation more accessible. In other cases, it may mean family leave benefits, phased retirement options, financial wellness programs, or tuition assistance. To be successful, work-life integration strategies must be relevant and responsive to the needs of all employees. One size does not fit all.

"Disability is part of the human experience yet many people see the medical label and assume individuals with disabilities 'can't' work, drive, live independently, etc. Let's turn that around, let's look at the 'can.'"

Kathleen West-Evans, Director of Business Relations, CSAVR

Who can help identify what those changes should be? The most significant source of knowledge around discriminatory policies is the people who are affected by them on a daily basis.

A rallying cry for the disability rights movement is "Nothing About Us Without Us," meaning that discussions pertaining to certain groups should be led by individuals *from* those groups, as it is their own exclusion that needs to be addressed. Seek out and listen to their perspectives first, learn where they need the most support, and then begin to make changes based on their needs and lived experiences.

Companies must conduct a candid assessment of current diversity and inclusion initiatives.

An important part of building a more inclusive workplace is assessing the good and bad of your current practices. All departments and teams must reflect on where bias might affect their policies, programs, and procedures and begin to collect constructive input on how to remedy weak spots.

 Download our curated list of tools at www.nonobviousdiversity.com/resources

While some may believe they have nothing to offer, inclusion—by its very definition—includes everyone. Whether a team member has been doing DEI work for years or is just now learning what equity means, their voice must be valued and heard. Make the effort to tell them that what they say matters.

What You Can Do . . .

As humans we can hesitate to embrace change even if that change has proven to be better for us in the long run.

"People are always frightened of change, but knowing people who look and operate differently is the most enriching experience for the workplace."

■ **Christina Ryan, Founder of Disability Leadership Institute Australia**

Conquering this fear starts by letting co-workers see that you value and honor their differences and view each of them as important.

Here are three action steps that each of us can take to foster more inclusivity and diversity in our own workplaces.

ACTION #1

Use your privilege to advocate for a colleague who might benefit from your support.

It can be easy for those who belong to social majorities to misunderstand the important role they can play as allies and advocates for diversity and inclusion. As a result, those least represented in our communities are disproportionately burdened with the task of fighting to be both represented and also heard.

Those with the least social capital and power shouldn't be asked to instigate the most change. The global #BlackLivesMatter movement provided a chance for those with privilege to openly acknowledge this fact, and many challenged themselves to use their positions of privilege to help someone who lacks it. Silence is no longer socially or professionally acceptable.

40% of LGBTQ employees are closeted at work.

Source: Boston Consulting Group, 2020

Moving forward, consider what more *you* could do at work to support those whose opinions and efforts are underappreciated or minimized. This might range from taking more opportunities during meetings to amplify a perspective from an undervalued colleague to inviting more underrepresented teammates to have a seat at the table in the first place.

"A champion . . . is someone who talks you up to others, someone who actively promotes your good work. The more you are able to champion other people's good stories, the better leader you become."

Beth Comstock, Author and Former Vice Chair of General Electric

If you have influence over recruiting and hiring practices, think also about what you can do to make job descriptions and the overall hiring process more inclusive of people from all backgrounds.

Broaden your recruiting pools and use non-obvious and innovative interviewing techniques.

When you think of diversifying candidate pools, the first tactic that might come to mind is setting a diversity quota. But that isn't always the best solution. Equity isn't about reducing people to numbers based on their identity.

As we mentioned earlier, traditional interview tactics can prevent some people from truly demonstrating their talents during the recruiting process. Even the language we include in almost every job description—strong communication skills, being a team player, having emotional intelligence, outgoing personality, the ability to network—can signal that only one type of person is welcome. Another powerful method for building a more inclusive workforce is looking to unlikely hiring sources when you seek to fill a role.

"Formerly incarcerated individuals have paid their debt to society . . . yet approximately 83 percent of employers don't openly hire people with felony convictions. In the United States, if you have a conviction history, there is no such thing as truly moving on with your life."

Susan Mason, CEO and Co-Founder of What's Next Washington

Cast a wider net: explore hiring more people with disabilities, veterans, and older workers; learn more about how to connect with and recruit formerly incarcerated talent and immigrants or refugees.

There are many national, regional, and community-based professional associations that are organized around the interests of each of these underrepresented communities. Developing relationships with them can provide important insight about non-traditional candidate pools, as well as inroads and opportunities to connect with them.

Every organization can benefit from considering applicants outside the usual sources, but doing so typically starts with a single bold choice from one hiring manager. What if that could be you?

ACTION #3

Embrace your vulnerability at work and practice greater emotional intelligence.

The value of soft skills has been misjudged in the past, as they've been deemed "too emotional" for the office. But our world is evolving every day, and leaders need to pivot as these become skills that are not only expected but necessary. The first step in that journey is embracing vulnerability, especially as we hope to change skeptical minds.

When people at all levels of leadership make this a priority, the workplace itself can become a more welcoming and open-minded atmosphere for people of all backgrounds to excel and bring their whole selves to work. Vulnerability among leaders creates a safe space for everyone else to feel that they can be vulnerable too. It's no wonder one recent survey showed that 76 percent of employees believe empathy drives productivity.[4]

"We cannot know everything. One of the biggest lessons I learned after joining my corporate board was the power of admitting I don't know. There is so much confidence that can come from openly doing that."

Lindsay Kaplan, Co-Founder of Chief

Jacqueline M. Baker, author and founder of leadership consultancy Scarlet Communications, offers a reminder that there's beauty in a leader's imperfection and humanity. "I look forward to leaders paving the way and being a good role model, which sometimes means saying, I don't know the answer to this," she says.

Next time you find yourself ill-equipped to answer a question, think of it not as a failure but as an opportunity to be vulnerable and learn something from someone else.

Beyond Diversity In
THE WORKPLACE

🏛 WHAT NEEDS TO HAPPEN:

- ❯ Leaders must recognize that great diversity exists within marginalized groups.

- ❯ Organizations need to listen to what people need and ensure those needs are met.

- ❯ Companies must conduct a candid assessment of current diversity and inclusion initiatives.

WHAT *YOU* CAN DO:

- ❯ Use your privilege to advocate for a colleague who might benefit from your support.

- ❯ Broaden your recruiting pools and use non-obvious and innovative interviewing techniques.

- ❯ Embrace your vulnerability at work and practice greater emotional intelligence.

💬 CONVERSATION STARTERS:

- ❯ In your workplace, what team members lack representation and what are 2-3 things you could do to correct this imbalance?

- ❯ What external voices that offer a different perspective could you bring in either as consultants or testers to offer a new lens on the work you do?

BEYOND DIVERSITY IN
TECHNOLOGY

"I don't have a feeling of inferiority. Never had.
I'm as good as anybody, but no better."
— *Katherine Johnson, NASA Mathematician*

Chapter Summary:

The tech industry has historically lacked representation from women, non-binary individuals, people of color and those with physical or mental disabilities. One result has been biased products and algorithms that affect everything from getting hired to securing a loan. To change this reality, more diverse talent pipelines must be built and marginalized voices within tech organizations must be elevated.

How It Is . . .

In the second half of 2019, Apple officially entered into the competitive financial services market by launching the Apple Card, which they described with their usual marketing hyperbole as "the most successful credit card launch ever."[1]

Behind the scenes, things were not so perfect.

The trouble began a few months after launch, when Danish programmer and tech entrepreneur David Heinemeier Hansson posted a series of tweets that subsequently went viral. In his first, he wrote:

"The @AppleCard is such a f----- sexist program. My wife and I filed joint tax returns, live in a community-property state, and have been married for a long time. Yet Apple's black box algorithm thinks I deserve 20x the credit limit she does. No appeals work."

Two days later, Apple co-founder Steve Wozniak tweeted that he and his wife had received similarly sexist credit assessments. More consumers reported the same problems. Despite the growing controversy, Apple continued to insist there was no discrimination in the algorithm that made these determinations. Legislators and the general public weren't convinced.

As global media covered the escalating story, journalists started seeking out other recent examples of algorithmic bias. They weren't hard to find.

Just a few weeks earlier, a study published in *Science* magazine found that the algorithms used by US hospitals to determine proper care for over 200 million patients were systematically discriminating against Black people.[2]

Microsoft had launched a chatbot that quickly became racist after assimilating public Twitter conversations. Multiple recruiting algorithms were shown to undervalue the résumés of women, people who were assigned female at birth, and people of color. These examples are just a few of many fueling the debate about the potential dangers of technology as a force for institutionalizing discrimination and inequity. The issue is often defined by the term used to describe it: *algorithmic bias*. This puts the blame on the algorithm itself, rather than the teams behind it.

Our focus on holding algorithms accountable may be a large part of the problem, according to Heather Krause, founder and principal data scientist at We All Count. Instead, Krause suggests we place more of our focus on those *programming* the algorithms and the leaders within organizations deciding which algorithms to develop and deploy in the first place.

Hansson shared a similar perspective after his experience with the Apple Card: "Apple has handed the customer experience and their reputation as an inclusive organization over to a biased, sexist algorithm it does not understand, cannot reason with, and is unable to control."

Rethinking the teams of people responsible for making technology and innovations more inclusive is not just a mental or philanthropic exercise in creating a more equitable world. History shows that neglecting this issue can have *very* real life or death consequences.

One notorious example comes from the 1960s, when seat belts were first developed by all-male engineering teams and introduced as a standard feature in cars. The original designs were based on the size of an average man, which meant that for *decades* afterward, women were 47 percent more likely to be seriously injured in a car crash.

Shockingly enough, it was only in the past decade that crash test dummies based on the female body started to be used in safety testing.[3]

Another concerning example of AI bias is the COMPAS (Correctional Offender Management Profiling for Alternative Sanctions) algorithm[4] used in court systems to predict the likelihood of criminal recidivism. The model predicted twice as many false positives for recidivism for Black offenders (45 percent) as it did for White offenders (23 percent).

Incidents like the Apple Card, automotive seat belt failures, or COMPAS raise serious questions about the negative impact of bias in technology. Because algorithms are essentially omnipresent nowadays, addressing this issue has become even more urgent.

We can start by finding ways to build a more inclusive pipeline of talent in all areas of the tech industry, including product development teams, data scientists, ethical/fairness review boards, and all higher leadership levels as well. This was one of several priorities and opportunities we discussed during our summit. From these conversations, a powerful vision for the future in the tech sector emerged.

How Things Are Changing . . .

Joy Buolamwini, a Ghanaian American computer scientist, researcher, and digital activist working at the Massachusetts Institute of Technology (MIT) Media Lab, realized the repercussions of algorithmic bias in our society as a postgraduate student.

While she conducted an engineering project, facial analysis software struggled to detect Buolamwini's face . . . until she put on a White mask. Right away, she knew this was more than a technical blunder. Rather than ignore her own concerns as a woman of color, she decided to explore the issue and lead a fight to address it.

35% of facial recognition errors happen when identifying dark skinned women. Only 1% happen with White males.

Source: Algorithmic Justice League (AJL)

In 2016, she started the Algorithmic Justice League (AJL)[5] to "raise awareness about the impacts of AI, equip advocates with empirical research to bolster campaigns, amplify the voices of the most impacted communities, and galvanize researchers, policymakers, and industry practitioners to mitigate algorithmic bias and harms."[6]

Her work, alongside that of others working in the field, inspired the hit Netflix documentary *Coded Bias,* which provided viewers with a glimpse of how artificial intelligence can impact our everyday lives.

"The troubling thing about data is that, if you're Black, it's likely to contain lies about you . . . to have accuracy calculated in the absence of my lived experience not only offends me, but also puts me in real danger."[7]

Inioluwa Deborah Raji, Computer Scientist and Mozilla Fellow

Not all technology is biased, thankfully. In fact, there has been significant progress in developing tech solutions to uncover and address bias in many areas of our lives. One example is VRperspectives, a training company that leverages digital storytelling to immerse people in realistic workplace scenarios and to allow them to actually feel the impact of exclusion.

As Myra LalDin, the company's founder, explains: "We are shining a spotlight on the things that are occurring daily that our brains often fail to notice."

Sometimes it's the very effort to recruit a more inclusive team that may expose hiring bias. Back in 2015, a single recruiting billboard ad from a Silicon Valley tech firm called OneLogin unintentionally sparked a movement. The ad featured an engineer from their team named Isis Anchalee with a real quote about how she loved her team and job.

Almost immediately, people online picked apart everything from the smile on Anchalee's face to the assumption that the brand must have used a stock photo instead of a real engineer. Isis didn't fit their preconceived notions of how an engineer should look.

 To see an image of the full billboard, visit www.nonobviousdiversity.com/resources

The controversy forced Anchalee into a spotlight she didn't ask for, but she decided to shift the conversation by posting a photo of herself with the hashtag #ilooklikeanengineer.[8] Thousands of others used the same hashtag to share their own stories of being marginalized or judged unfairly while working in the tech sector. These widely known challenges have inspired the formation of many groups who are working to address the lack of representation in the sector and build a more diverse talent pipeline.

For example, Girls Who Code is a nonprofit organization with over 8,500 programs worldwide working to close the gender gap in technology by increasing the number of women in computer science.

Tangible outcomes of this push for more women-led teams and startups founded by underrepresented tech entrepreneurs are beginning to emerge.

Startups like Bumble (a dating app that lets women make the first move), Blendoor (an anonymized recruiting app that hides gender and race to prevent unconscious bias) and Textio (an "augmented writing" platform that helps automatically correct biased language in writing) were all started by female founders. More importantly, they are all using more inclusive teams to put the needs of previously ignored groups at the center of their products and missions.[9]

The success of these platforms is a positive sign, but these types of examples remain far too rare.

The tech industry has a long way to go before marginalized groups are adequately represented and their perspectives are valued, respected and properly compensated.

"Technology should be used as an opportunity to advance inclusion and the disability community. Many of us have been advocating for work from home, flexible environments and the pandemic has helped enable that."

Tiffany Yu, Entrepreneur and Disability Rights Advocate

What Needs To Happen . . .

One place where the change needs to start is in pay equity. A study in early 2021 titled the "Racial and Gender Pay Scorecard" determined that most of the top technology companies in the world still score poorly on their willingness and ability to address the gender and racial pay gap at their organizations.[10] Even more concerning, the strides made in bringing different people into the tech industry are often short-lived.

Just four years after sparking her hashtag movement, Isis Anchalee admitted to feeling burnt out from the Silicon Valley lifestyle and announced she would be leaving to start a social impact company instead.[11] Anchalee is not alone; even in those companies that have made progress in hiring more diversely, turnover continues to be high and creating a culture of inclusion and belonging remains elusive.

56% of women in the technology sector drop out mid-career due to negative workplace experiences.

Source: National Center for Women In Technology

What will it take for a more inclusive pipeline of talent to create a generational shift in how diverse the tech industry itself can be, and for this diversity to be reflected through the products and services that we all increasingly rely on? Here are a few suggestions.

Foster a culture of inclusion within tech teams.

The gender disparity in tech is one of the most glaring representations of inequity in the US labor force. To list yet another startling statistic, tech companies are interviewing exclusively male candidate pools for open positions 41 percent of the time, versus exclusively female candidate pools only 4 percent of the time.[12] Workers who identify as LGBTQ+ are presumably even more rare—though it's impossible to know for sure due to a lack of available data on the question. This isn't a skills issue, but rather one of structural barriers to entry and a widespread culture of exclusion and homogeneity.

"We need to be more aggressive in thinking about what will attract more people into tech of all very different backgrounds, sooner versus later."

Brenda Darden Wilkerson, CEO of Anitab.org

To address these issues, leaders in tech need to set meaningful representation goals, particularly at the decision making level, continually reevaluate the climate of their work environments, pinpoint pay and opportunity inequities and set clear policies related to harassment, discrimination and microaggression at work. If you want to make your workplace more welcoming, you can start by reformatting the rules of entry and the laws of membership, both spoken and unspoken.

A great first step in doing this may be to go beyond numbers and instead really listen to employees. For example, interview data can be collected on why workers from particular backgrounds seem to leave the company. Why is only one type of employee being promoted on a consistent basis? What factors drive engagement and disengagement? How do these differ across employee groups?

Candid questions, asked through anonymized feedback processes that protect respondents from any internal retribution, are a good start. Organizations can also assemble a DEI-centric task force to act on employee feedback and bring in a DEI-focused leader with the institutional power and remit to make changes happen.

IMPERATIVE #2

Reconsider hiring criteria and prioritize diverse perspectives.

A few years ago, you'd be hard-pressed to find a job opening in tech that didn't require several advanced degrees and a slew of technical skills.

This can present a serious barrier for candidates from backgrounds underrepresented in tech, or those with more non-traditional backgrounds, who may already feel ill-qualified to pursue their passion for technology on account of these differences.

Though recruiters have slowly begun to open their minds to a broader range of identities and career paths, even today most openings come with high expectations around a generic (and often arbitrary) list of skills or degrees.

As author and longtime Google employee Alana Karen notes, "technical knowledge is not supreme to everything else." She is the author of *The Adventures of Women In Tech*, a book that features interviews with women who paved the way for greater diversity in tech—and what that means for future generations.

"You don't have to be an engineering student to be successful in tech . . . . we need to stop and think about our criteria and what is really required to be successful."

Kate Isler, CEO of The W Marketplace

While there must be many paths to building a successful career in technology, it is important to address the mistaken belief that bringing in team members with different backgrounds or credentials somehow *lowers* the bar for talent. This is a damaging and false perception. No one is advocating for bringing in people who aren't competent or qualified.

We are, however, advocating for the assessment of potential teammates based on their actual abilities and skills, instead of whether they have a degree from a desirable school or can list a past corporate role doing a similar job on their résumé.

Demand transparency around technology and ethics.

Experts agree: unbiased algorithms are impossible. Rather than seeking to make the technology perfect, we must strive toward being more deliberate and strategic in the identities of the creators of the technology, the situations where we employ algorithms, and in how exclusively we rely on them. An algorithm, at least for the foreseeable future, is not a substitute for thoughtful human judgment.

To ensure algorithms do not discriminate against or disparage vulnerable groups, we also need to demand that the technology industry be more transparent around how algorithms are designed, developed, and distributed, as well as who is working on them.

To that end, in 2019 a group of AI experts crowdsourced an algorithmic bill of rights,[13] which centered consent and accountability as potential pillars for future software development. Initiatives like this spotlight the potential for external, independent review processes to take place, and highlight the importance of tracking an algorithm's influence over time and offering a public forum for those affected, as well as allies for underrepresented identities, to voice concerns.

What You Can Do . . .

The tech sector has a far-reaching impact on our future lives and society, so the fight for more inclusive teams is urgent and essential.

In part, this is a recruiting and talent pipeline challenge that can be addressed through more inclusive and open-minded recruitment and hiring practices. The broader challenge is to spotlight and address systemic, sometimes unintentional biases designed into the products and services we use.

Below are some actionable suggestions that can help you face both of these challenges in your personal and professional life.

ACTION #1

Start mentoring a junior professional from an underrepresented group.

Inviting more underrepresented and marginalized groups into tech is a gateway that will help us face many other challenges, but it will fail to have an impact if we don't intentionally support and mentor these colleagues. To grow a diverse talent pipeline, leaders and managers alike can mentor or sponsor a junior professional of color or another underrepresented identity. Such relationships can bring greater attention to diverse talent in the organization and create more equitable pathways to advancement.

"Our champions come from different places. Sponsors are mentor figures who must go beyond offering guidance and instead act as advocates by using their social capital to further the careers of others."

Dwana Franklin-Davis, CEO of Reboot Representation

If you aren't someone with positional power, there are still valuable actions you can take. For starters, you can advocate for or volunteer with education initiatives that specifically aid the development of more inclusive workforces in technology.

You can also spread the word about existing diverse tech leaders by signal-boosting their work (e.g., sharing their blogs and social posts, attending their speaking engagements, buying their books).

ACTION #2

Demand more inclusive tech teams, whether you work in the industry or just interact with it.

Racism and sexism aren't the only forms of discrimination keeping people out of tech. They routinely operate hand in hand with ageism, ableism, classism, transphobia, and other prejudices.

If you are in a hiring position, you must consider intersectionality during recruitment and hiring, tenure and retention, mobility and promotion rates, succession planning, and more. When observing these processes, look beyond the typical (albeit important) issues of gender and race. Consider ability, socioeconomic class, religion, communication style, educational background, citizenship, etc., and determine whether these dimensions are overlooked or unfairly handled in the context of organizational systems.

And as a consumer and user of technology, consider what platforms and tools you support and whether the people behind them believe in similar ideals.

ACTION #3

Be more aware of daily examples of algorithmic bias and call out inequities when you see them.

Algorithmic bias and the myriad threats it poses to the future of equity in our society are hard to overstate. Yet for every case of an infuriated husband calling out gender bias in credit scores or a flawed system that incorrectly predicts criminal recidivism for Black offenders, there are hundreds of other examples of algorithmic bias that go ignored and uncorrected.

The only way to enact change is if we have more people that notice and are willing to speak up. Voices like yours.

The more people who know about bias in technology, the more vigilant we can become in spotting it. When we finally reach critical mass, our demands for greater accountability will be undeniable.

Beyond Diversity In
TECHNOLOGY

 ## WHAT NEEDS TO HAPPEN:

- Foster a culture of inclusion within tech teams.
- Reconsider hiring criteria and prioritize diverse perspectives.
- Demand transparency around technology and ethics.

WHAT *YOU* CAN DO:

- Start mentoring a junior professional from an underrepresented group.
- Demand more inclusive tech teams, whether you work in the industry or just interact with it.
- Be more aware of daily examples of algorithmic bias and call out inequities when you see them.

CONVERSATION STARTERS:

- Challenge yourself to discover 2-3 reasons why the stories that appear at the top of your social media feed or your Google search results rise to the top. What does this teach you about how the algorithms work?
- What are some technology platforms developed by inclusive teams or started by underrepresented founders that you can support or switch to using?

BEYOND DIVERSITY IN
ENTREPRENEURSHIP

"Whatever you do, be different—that was the advice my mother gave me, and I can't think of better advice for an entrepreneur. If you're different, you will stand out."

— Anita Roddick, Founder of The Body Shop

Chapter Summary:

People from marginalized groups have often started their own ventures as a response to workplace discrimination, but these entrepreneurs frequently lack adequate funding or access to support networks. Making entrepreneurship more inclusive will require increased access to capital, active local support networks and well-funded accelerator programs.

How It Is . . .

In 2016, two researchers from the Vienna University of Economics and Business penned an article for the *Harvard Business Review* that posed a provocative question: Are immigrants more entrepreneurial?[1]

The question was inspired by an experiment where a team of venture capitalists and experts were asked to rate the potential of a list of entrepreneurial ideas, and found that ideas from people who had "cross-cultural experience" received significantly higher ratings than those from applicants with more culturally isolated backgrounds.

Published just months before former President Donald Trump took office in the United States, the authors of the study wryly concluded that "public money may be better spent on building incubators for migrant entrepreneurs than on building border walls."[2]

The comment underscores the tension that has long existed between the opportunities entrepreneurship represents and the reality of who ends up prospering from them. Despite the many ways that the world's nations have frequently benefitted from an influx of global talent through immigration, a resurgence of xenophobia and racist beliefs from both elected officials and their constituents has resulted in potential immigrants being depicted as undesirable outsiders.

Multiple studies show great economic value in courting and nurturing these entrepreneurs, but the truth is that immigrants and people from other underrepresented groups may turn to entrepreneurship in *response* to the discrimination they face in the traditional job market and corporate workplace.[3]

Across the world, immigrant founders looking to start over in a foreign country are often forced to create their own employment opportunities without an established support network. In this sense, entrepreneurship is not purely an expression of ambition, but also a tactic for economic survival.

Perhaps due to this common situation, research suggests immigrants are almost twice as likely to become entrepreneurs as native-born citizens in many countries.[4]

Yet it isn't just immigrant minorities who are starting businesses. For more than twenty years, the Global Entrepreneurship Monitor (GEM) has tracked the rise of entrepreneurship, and after a difficult pandemic year of 2020 where hundreds of thousands of entrepreneurs closed their businesses, the following year experienced a global resurgence— particularly among older entrepreneurs aged 55-65, women, and people of color.[5]

Over half of all new businesses started in the United States are by minority business owners.

Source: US Senate Committee on Small Business and Entrepreneurs

In the United States alone, NPR reported that Americans were starting businesses in 2021 at the fastest rate in more than a decade.[6] While all of this activity isn't solely due to underrepresented entrepreneurs, it is tempting to see entrepreneurship as the great equalizer to long-standing workplace inequities.

More than half of young entrepreneurs, for example, consider age bias to be a factor in why they became entrepreneurs.[7] For the past decade, the GEM report has also consistently shown that older entrepreneurs are one of the fastest growing cohorts. In some countries, people with disabilities have a higher rate of entrepreneurship than those without.[8]

"There's an unfortunate side of some people with disabilities becoming self-employed freelance entrepreneurs because there's a lack of opportunity and inclusion in the workplace."

Martyn Sibley, Co-Founder and CEO of Purple Goat Agency

One recent study even concluded that high-net-worth female entrepreneurs could *reverse* the gender pay gap, earning 14 percent more than their male peers.[9]

All these statistics offer a positive view of the life-changing act of empowerment that becoming an entrepreneur can be for some people from underrepresented groups—but this isn't a universal truth. Many of these entrepreneurs still face an uphill battle to grow their businesses, and may also suffer from the lifestyle demands that can come from being an entrepreneur.

In other words, entrepreneurship has a dark side.

For one thing, many successful business owners tend to glorify their lifestyle of constant work, relentless positivity, and never-ending "life hacking" to optimize every slice of every day and night. Even "sleep hacking"—where you quantify and optimize your sleep—has become a rapidly growing industry.

This so-called "hustle culture" is simultaneously idolized and criticized—but there is relatively little discussion about how this 24/7 concept of work excludes or disadvantages certain groups of people, such as older workers, those with caregiving responsibilities toward children or aging parents, or those with physical disabilities.

Based on who we see celebrated in the media, our perception of successful entrepreneurs also tends to be skewed toward young, tech-savvy White males. Ironically, this is in spite of the fact that the data regularly offers evidence that the assumptions behind these biases are flawed.

Companies with a female founder performed 63% better than investments with all-male founding teams.

Source: First Round Capital

A study by First Round Capital, for example, demonstrated that companies with female founders outperformed those with all-male founding teams by 63 percent.[10] Despite reports like this, the chances of a woman or entrepreneur of color getting funded have long been far less than the chances of funding for White male entrepreneurs. This inequity is steadily becoming more visible, thanks to the efforts of advocacy groups and the underfunded entrepreneurs themselves. As a result, there are more efforts today than ever before to try and address the problem.

How Things Are Changing . . .

This shift offers us the ideal topic to begin exploring how entrepreneurship is changing: access to funding. To better understand this topic, let's go behind the scenes with one of the voices working to make venture capital funding more widely available.

Ever since his parents bought him a Commodore 64 computer, Marlon Nichols showed a burgeoning interest in technology. His father worked as a train engineer in Jamaica before the family moved to New York, where his mother worked as a housekeeper until she got a beautician license and opened her own shop. From a young age, Marlon witnessed firsthand the value of ambition, hard work, and entrepreneurship.

That upbringing led him to become the first member of his family to attend college, and eventually to focus his work on empowering and financing underinvested communities. Today Nichols is a founding managing partner of MaC Venture Capital, a seed-stage venture capital firm that made headlines for raising $110 million in March of 2021—one of the largest first-time fundraises by a majority Black-owned venture firm.

With 81 percent of their portfolio of companies having Black, Latinx, or women founders, Marlon and his fellow general partners are shifting the landscape of venture funding to make it more accessible to underrepresented founders.

They are not alone. While traditional financial institutions continue to underinvest in trailblazing leaders that come from diverse backgrounds, there are a growing number of new initiatives aimed at tackling this inequity. The W Fund, for example, is an investment firm focusing on fueling the startup ecosystem, aggregating capital, and deploying funds to women and startups that are driving the future of tech.

"We know that the next Jeff Bezos is going to be a woman or underrepresented founder, and we intend to fund them and see them through a major exit."

Allyson Kapin, Founding Partner at The W Fund

The nonprofit BLCK VC equips Black investors with the access, education, and community they need to accelerate their careers in venture capital. Vancouver-based Raven Indigenous Capital Partners provides impact investing to improve outcomes in Indigenous communities.

The larger venture capital community is also starting to make this a priority. In the UK, a nonprofit organization called Diversity VC created a new certification standard for the industry to measure which VC firms are actively investing in diverse founders and bringing in diverse talent. Alongside industry-wide standards, large venture capital firms like Intel Capital, Khosla Ventures and Kleiner Perkins are announcing their own initiatives to seek out underrepresented founders.

Of course, funding is just the start. To encourage more diversity in entrepreneurship, we must support a growing arsenal of recommended networks, government-funded support systems, co-working spaces, and mentorship opportunities as well.

In researching this book, we examined a range of accelerator programs, networking groups, and mentoring communities. These groups are now funding grants and education programs that are so varied and numerous that we catalogued all of them— segmented by identity, industry, and geography—and published the list as an online resource.

 Download our list of professional networks, funding groups, educational opportunities, and more at www.nonobviousdiversity.com/resources

What Needs To Happen . . .

Encouraging and empowering more diversity in entrepreneurship will require a combination of both public and private initiatives focused on the dual challenge of providing access to capital *and* building the support networks, funding groups, educational opportunities and more that enable a steady flow of successful businesses to emerge, rather than an occasional success story.

Through a combination of insights gathered from our summit, we put together a roadmap that shows what it will take to make meaningful change happen.

IMPERATIVE #1

The broader investment community must ensure teams making funding decisions are diverse and inclusive.

In situations where investors fail to make significant bets on diverse startup founders, it can be a problem of unconscious bias.

Research has shown that the venture investing teams most likely to fund diverse founders tend to be diverse themselves.[11] Investing teams comprising more than one gender are 2 times more likely to invest in gender-diverse founding teams, for example, 2.6 times more likely to invest in women-led entrepreneur teams, and over 3 times more likely to invest in a female CEO.[12] Alternatively, studies have shown that homogenous teams suffer, limiting their potential as businesses: venture capital teams with shared ethnicity have 5.8 percent lower success rates, and those with shared educational backgrounds have 11.5 percent lower success rates.[13]

Although inclusive leadership teams within the financial community won't solve discriminatory funding practices entirely, it is a practical and impactful way of improving the odds that capital gets into the capable hands of communities who have been historically deprived of it in the past.

— IMPERATIVE #2 —

Networks for aspiring entrepreneurs must be created to help address systemic barriers to success.

The K'é Main Street Learning Lab in Mesa, Arizona is a small business incubator space founded with the mission of highlighting the leadership that exists within business leaders in marginalized groups who are rarely visible to the broader business community. As co-founder and business coach Pamela Slim says, it was necessary because "despite mountains of evidence about the benefits of diversity, and decades of advocacy for inclusive and equitable startup spaces, most incubator programs were dominated by White males."

For the past several years, K'é (named for a Diné word meaning "system of kinship") has provided a home for hundreds of startup leaders of color looking for an inclusive space to teach and mentor their community to get their business ideas off the ground. Organizations like this offer resources, support, and guidance to entrepreneurs in local communities around the world.

Networks like the Learning Lab are crucial to future successes and are always a core part of any city-wide revitalization effort around the world. Each of these is the equivalent of planting seeds in a professional field. The regions that do invest in these types of programs are likely to not only create more economic prosperity locally, but also attract more diverse talent to the area.

IMPERATIVE #3

Diversity must be reframed as a competitive advantage rather than a barrier to overcome.

Travis Holoway is the co-founder and CEO of SoLo Funds, a mobile platform that provides more affordable access to loans. As a Black entrepreneur, he's all too familiar with the struggle to get ahead in the face of systemic barriers.

"It's been tough, and we constantly have this feeling of being a little bit underestimated and undervalued," Holoway describes. "But on the flip side, it's actually made us stronger as a company. At the end of the day, when we finally get to the point of raising the capital, we're typically a more structurally sound business."

Entrepreneur, investor, and co-founder of Tech.co, Established and Established Ventures, Frank Gruber shares a similar perspective: "If you can find the strength in your background, it can become a superpower." By focusing on the positive, entrepreneurs in all industry sectors can find a unique way to stand apart.

"A diverse mix of voices leads to better discussions, decisions, and outcomes for everyone."

— **Sundar Pichai, CEO of Google**

If entire industries can start to see this "superpower" in business people from varied backgrounds, diverse entrepreneurs can more easily overcome any initial rejections and find a home for their business ideas to succeed.

What You Can Do . . .

Eliminating bias and discrimination from the global landscape of entrepreneurship is a big challenge. At the same time, there is no economic equalizer that can have quite the same impact in creating a more inclusive world as granting *all* entrepreneurs the opportunity to achieve prosperity—for both themselves and their communities.

Whether you consider yourself part of an underrepresented group or not—and whether you are an entrepreneur or not—a world where more people from diverse backgrounds can make their business ideas successful is a better world for us all. So, let's take a look at what you personally can do to help make this vision a reality.

Spend your money and social capital on finding and supporting marginalized entrepreneurs.

The challenge that many entrepreneurs face, first and foremost, is one of awareness. Newer professionals or freelancers have a similar challenge of breaking into industries without access to the same network of door-opening colleagues that others may have.

The only way these entrepreneurs and professionals can succeed is if more established professionals in positions of power or privilege choose to invest in them, and find the courage to put their own reputations on the line to recommend them to others.

What if all of us could do more to use whatever privilege we enjoy as motivation to move out of our comfort zone and be an ally to someone who could use our support?

This might start with choosing to buy products or services from diverse businesses. If you're an entrepreneur or have decision-making power at a company, you might also do this on behalf of an organization by seeking out diverse vendors and suppliers. The bottom line is, buying and recommending with intention is one of the best, most actionable ways to support diversity in entrepreneurship.

Seek out less visible and underutilized forms of support, advice, and funding.

Despite some of the pioneering organizations we featured in this chapter, mainstream venture capitalism remains an industry with gross levels of inequity. Aside from those few dedicated innovators who are trying to change this reality, there is a vast world of fundraising outside of traditional Silicon Valley-based VC sources.

The problem is, non-traditional fundraising isn't always easy to find or access. Aspiring entrepreneurs can be tempted to seek out mentors and advisors who are only familiar with the entrenched, existing systems of funding and networking. As a result, they can easily get steered down a path that will require struggling to overcome systemic barriers. The narrative is built on the assumption that entrepreneurial success for any business owner inherently requires conquering all of these things and persevering.

Instead, what about bypassing these barriers by engaging with alternative networks populated with investors or mentors who come from similar backgrounds? There is power in surrounding yourself with people who share your aspirations and upbringing, rather than always being the solitary voice from a different background in a room filled with people who, though often well-intentioned, are unlikely to understand your unique journey or share your values.

This kind of alternative funding is possible through angel funds such as Goldenseeds (focused on high-potential, women-led businesses) and Gaingels (a network seeking to create social change through business by investing in the best companies that embrace LGBTQ+ leadership).

"I'm a part of various groups of female founders, whether it be BIPOC, tech-enabled CEOs, or Black female founders who have been VC-backed . . . and it feels like the network is expanding."

Courtney Caldwell, Co-Founder of ShearShare

This approach—the strategy of seeking out more empathetic avenues and networks—can extend to funding, banking, networking groups, mentors, and just about any other aspect of support that an entrepreneur might need while building a business from the ground up.

ACTION #3

Invest more of your time and engagement in cross-cultural thinking.

Austrian billionaire Dietrich Mateschitz famously approached Chaleo Yoovidhya, the original creator of a Thai drink known to local truck drivers as Krating Daeng after trying it for himself and realizing it cured his jet lag. The drink, originally promoted as a way for factory workers and truck drivers to make it through long shifts, was the inspiration for what would later be rebranded as Red Bull.

The world of entrepreneurship is filled with legendary origin stories like this.

Each is an example of a business started by an entrepreneur willing to look beyond their own home culture and engage in cross-cultural thinking. The lesson taught by these stories is simple: adopting a more diverse and inclusive point of view is key to developing a brilliant and innovative concept or to making your existing concept stand out from the crowd and appeal to a wider consumer base. Traveling is one way to build cross-cultural awareness. Another is to actively seek out conversations and opportunities with people who come from backgrounds that differ significantly from your own.

Beyond Diversity In
ENTREPRENEURSHIP

🏛 WHAT NEEDS TO HAPPEN:

- The broader investment community must ensure teams making funding decisions are diverse and inclusive.
- Networks for aspiring entrepreneurs must be created to help address systemic barriers to success.
- Diversity must be reframed as a competitive advantage rather than a barrier to overcome.

WHAT *YOU* CAN DO:

- Spend your money and social capital on finding and supporting marginalized entrepreneurs.
- Seek out less visible and underutilized forms of support, advice, and funding.
- Invest more of your time and engagement in cross-cultural thinking.

💬 CONVERSATION STARTERS:

- Consider the stores or businesses that you buy from regularly. What more could you do to seek out and buy from more diverse businesses?
- What are three actionable ways in which you can meet diverse, non-traditional entrepreneurs in business and consider working with them?

BEYOND DIVERSITY IN
LEADERSHIP

"We can't pray or wish for diversity. We need intervention, attention, mentoring and development of those minorities to ensure all are represented in our organizations."

— *Indra Nooyi, Former CEO of PepsiCo*

Chapter Summary:

Although there has been growing attention on the need to diversify our workplaces, commitment to change at the leadership level has been slow. The majority of CEOs and top leadership executives remain largely male, older and White. Changing this reality will take a combination of organizational commitments, more equitable workplaces and targeted development programs.

How It Is . . .

Most people will never know the experience of belonging to a privileged group and then having that status taken away overnight. Natalie Egan is not like most people.

At age 39, after stepping down as CEO of her first major start-up she realized her true identity and came out as a transgender woman to her wife and children. Like almost all trans and gender non-conforming people, her journey hasn't been easy. She has lost friends, family, and opportunities while receiving almost non-stop media attention in the months after her transition.

Her experience, though difficult, inspired her to start Translator, Inc., an "empathy software company" that helps teams and leaders navigate exactly the sort of difficult conversations she had to endure when first coming out as a trans woman.

While her personal story is one of a leader experiencing a powerful moment of self-awakening, the efforts of her company—and dozens of others like it—are helping to create the momentum for leaders from companies of all sizes to bridge the growing "empathy gap," for themselves.

To better understand this empathy gap, let's consider some numbers. According to the 2020 State of Workplace Empathy report by Business Solver, while 76 percent of employees believe an organization's empathy drives productivity, only 52 percent of CEOs agree. In addition, just 45 percent of employees view

CEOs in general as empathetic, versus 87 percent of CEOs themselves. When leaders lack the self-awareness to understand the limitations of their own life experiences, they rarely develop true empathy for the people they are leading. As a result, already marginalized team members continue to be excluded from the workplace.

"I had been living my life in a bubble of White male privilege with access and resources . . . and all of a sudden, I was an overnight minority. I experienced bias, discrimination, and hatred for the first time in my life. Prior to that, I never had to think about my identity. I'd never been not accepted for who I was."

Natalie Egan, CEO of Translator

The growing focus on diversity and inclusion in companies, governments, and many other institutions has fueled the urgent need to bring more empathy to all levels of management. One way this is being implemented is by formalizing roles and teams dedicated to the work of creating a diverse and inclusive company culture. The appointing of "Chief Diversity Officers" (CDOs), for example, is one highly visible choice meant to spearhead the push to make the organizations they work for more diverse, equitable, and inclusive on every level.

But even with the growing numbers of appointed leaders tasked with focusing on DEI, actually achieving representation and inclusive cultures remains a daunting task. When it comes to representation, we need only examine the business world at large to see a discouraging lack of diversity amongst the global ranks of leadership.

Almost 90 percent of Fortune 500 CEOs are *still* White men. On the *Forbes* real-time list of the 100 richest billionaires, the top 10 slots are predominantly occupied by White men. A joint survey by Leanin.org and McKinsey found that only 34 percent of senior management roles were filled by women, a number that dips as low as 21 percent when narrowed down to only the VP, SVP, and C-level roles.[1]

28% of managerial positions were held by women globally in 2019. This is nearly the same proportion as in 1995.

Source: United Nations World's Women Report 2020

Though recent projections estimate that the number of women and people of color on Fortune 100 and 500 boards is on track to increase to 40 percent by 2024,[2] this is a misleading data point as merely adding a single woman or person of color to a board already populated by a dozen White male voices should not be celebrated as a success story. Instead, it should be welcomed as a starting point and represents the bare minimum of progress. If corporate boards symbolize the pinnacle of senior leadership, they paint a sobering picture of how far we still have left to go.

For example, the number of women in senior management roles worldwide as of 2020 was still only 29 percent.[3] Correcting a gender imbalance years in the making—exacerbated by a global pandemic where an estimated 865,000 women left their jobs in the month of September 2020 alone—will require unprecedented and proactive action on the part of today's leaders. David G. Smith and W. Brad Johnson have written extensively about what male leaders can do to tackle this challenge. As sociology and psychology professors respectively, they published a book in 2020 titled *Good Guys: How Men Can Be Better Allies for Women in the Workplace.* In it they share the perspective that building a more equitable workplace must begin with men recognizing their privilege.

There are literally hundreds of "every-man perks," they describe, from being less likely to be interrupted to people automatically assuming you know what you're talking about. To be better allies for women, aside from the obvious leadership priorities of promoting and mentoring female leaders, they also suggest specifically seeking out honest feedback from women. As Pulitzer Prize-winning presidential historian Doris Kearns Goodwin once wrote, "Good leadership requires you to surround yourself with people of diverse perspectives who can disagree with you without fear of retaliation."

What was once dispassionately described as managing "human resources" is slowly being reimagined into a different sort of leadership role, focused less on squeezing more productivity out of workers, and more on creating a sense of belonging and a feeling of being seen and heard. Often, this starts with something as simple and symbolic as a job title. Claude Silver, for example, is the "Chief Heart Officer" at Vayner Media, a role she crafted with CEO Gary Vaynerchuck to focus on creating an environment of psychological safety for all team members to feel engaged.

"Diversity is a fact, but inclusion is a choice we make every day. As leaders, we have to put out the message that we embrace and not just tolerate diversity."

Nellie Borrero, Managing Director, Global Inclusion and Diversity, Accenture

Making this shift means senior leaders in all divisions of a business must also step up and create change by going beyond performative allyship (corporate gifts or superficial statements of support). The real work of addressing systemic biases and acknowledging what has caused harm in the past also requires that we each examine our own role in that harm, whether explicit or complicit.

This type of awakening is hard to achieve, but a good place to start is by identifying and candidly discussing the times when bias may have happened, and how it might be addressed in the future.

"Vulnerability is the least celebrated emotion in our society."

Mohadesa Najumi, Writer and Social Scientist

How Things Are Changing . . .

In 2005, Turkish immigrant Hamdi Ulukaya founded the Greek-style yogurt producer Chobani LLC. The inspiration to launch a yogurt company came from his childhood, which he spent raising sheep and goats and making cheese with his family. From that humble past, a runaway success was born: in less than five years, Chobani realized over $1 billion in annual sales and became the leading seller of Greek yogurt in America.

In addition to providing an inspiring story about the triumph and resilience of the immigrant experience, Ulukaya has introduced some industry-shifting ideas as well. In 2016, he famously announced that every one of his 2000 employees at every level would receive shares in the company. As they allotted shares to employees based on tenure, some of the company's lowest-ranking employees became millionaires overnight.

"[The leadership goal at Chobani is to] let people be themselves, and if you have a cultural environment that welcomes everyone for who they are, it just works."

Hamdi Ulukaya, Founder of Chobani

In addition, Chobani has long offered a mandatory six-week parental leave for *all* parents (including those who adopt), and approximately 30 percent of employees at Chobani are resettled immigrants or refugees.

The environment Ulukaya seeks to foster is one we all hope to one day be a part of: a place where leaders prioritize empathy, psychological safety, financial equity, and true inclusion.

Organizations commonly hire leaders to focus on diversity but give them limited scope to enact real or meaningful change. Their impact, unsurprisingly, is therefore limited. At our summit, Veena Jayadeva shared how her current "Head of Corporate Social Responsibility" job title at insurance firm Guardian Life intentionally does not specifically mention diversity or inclusion.

As she notes, "I bring the diversity and inclusion piece to all the conversations I'm having. So it can be around sourcing and vendors; it can be around the talent pipeline; it can be around the everyday actions that employees can take to make our company a more inclusive place to work."

"Inclusion and fairness in the workplace . . . is not simply the right thing to do; it's the smart thing to do."

Alexis Herman, former US Secretary of Labor

Every department relies on humans to succeed, and every human individual relies on being included and welcomed to do their best work. Therefore, every department has a critical role to play in advancing equity and inclusion.

What Needs To Happen . . .

Today's global business news is rife with opinions about how individual leaders can create more inclusive teams, and how organizations should promote or hire leaders from underrepresented groups.

Some suggest that every company should have a chief diversity officer. Others believe efforts must start from the very top by making corporate boards of directors more diverse. Both approaches seem logical, but the truth is that creating a reality where leadership is more diverse and inclusive requires changes on an organizational, systemic, *and* individual level. And it requires commitment across the board.

IMPERATIVE #1

The "glass ceiling" cannot be replaced with the "glass cliff."

The metaphor of a "glass ceiling" has been used for years to describe the invisible barrier that prevents women and other underrepresented talent from rising to the highest ranks in an organization. In 2004, psychologists Michelle Ryan and Alex Haslam described the "glass cliff," a phenomenon where women are more likely than men to be promoted to leadership roles during periods of crisis or downturn, when the chance of failure is strongest.[4] The paradox is that many women see taking on such risky executive roles as their only opportunity to lead a company.

Oftentimes, the woman in charge is then scapegoated for the inevitable catastrophe and replaced by a more "traditional" (i.e., male) leader who is perceived as a savior. This isn't progress—it is sabotage.

The onus to fix a broken system should be on the broader collective of senior leaders who have the privilege and power to pave a safe path forward for successors.

"The level of pressure women of color feel to conform in their spaces is always surprising. Often people expect you to get along and be a certain way."

Deepa Purushothaman, Co-Founder of nFormation

If your organization seeks to create an environment where everyone has equitable opportunities to advance, structural changes need to be made so that high-potential diverse talent can rise without fear of being set up to fail. To address this, filter your leadership succession plans through an equity lens, and consider who is currently receiving experiential training.

Things like executive coaching, participation in highly visible projects, one-on-one sponsorships, and domain training are all places to embed an equity mindset. Does the makeup of your talent pool reflect the diversity of your audience and customers? Does it even reflect the diversity of your internal workforce? If the answer is no, greater effort needs to be allocated to fix that imbalance.

Mentorship must be available to all, not only a select few.

Within many companies, mentorship for rising leaders is only offered as a highly selective and desirable program available solely to the highest performing candidates. As a result, a tiny number of women or candidates of color get selected for this fast track to leadership candidacy. Rather than limiting such programs to only the top one percent of candidates, what if mentorship programs opened up and focused on helping *everyone* improve?

Denise Hamilton is a nationally recognized inclusion strategist and the founder of WatchHerWork, a digital platform for professional women. Hamilton says there is such a hunger for meaningful mentor relationships, especially among women, but that hunger goes unfulfilled. The fight to democratize professional development inspired WatchHerWork, which now offers a suite of services (including keynotes, executive coaching, leadership events, and digital courses) to help women go further faster.

The only way we can achieve a future where diverse talent thrives is by offering innovative leadership mentoring resources like these.

Diverse leadership cannot be treated as a "one and done" challenge.

For years the European Union has debated legislation that would require 40 percent of all corporate boards to be comprised of women. Already, many countries have legislation in place requiring that at least one board member be a woman.

According to the 2020 Women on Boards Gender Diversity Index, women now hold 22.6 percent of the board seats among the United States' largest publicly traded companies, and women are gaining seats at a faster rate than men. But progress is not happening at an equal pace across industries.

One-third of all companies in the US have either one or no women on their boards. Board members with disabilities are so rare, and the topic is so infrequently discussed, that one industry trade group felt the need to launch an awareness campaign to address the issue with the obvious but still sadly necessary tagline: "Diversity Includes Disability."[5]

This is the sort of double-edged progress we have become accustomed to when reviewing diversity in leadership across the globe. There is mounting pressure to include people from underrepresented groups in leadership roles, but many companies and governments even today place one candidate in a new role and congratulate themselves on a job well done.

Bringing more diversity into leadership ranks cannot be treated as an exercise in checking a box. As Jennifer regularly advocates, a better practice is to aim for the "rule of three"—where you have at least three leaders from marginalized groups who join a particular team or corporate board. This offers a critical level of representation where diverse individuals can be seen as more than just a token hire or solitary voice, but it only works if there is an inclusive environment that embraces these individuals once they do agree to join.

What You Can Do . . .

Being a leader looks different for everyone, but in the literal sense of the term, a leader is someone whom others follow. An *inclusive* leader nurtures purpose in others—particularly those who have struggled to be seen, heard, and valued—and addresses their own knowledge gaps and biases on a regular basis.

As we look ahead to the future of leadership, especially within the DEI space, here are some things we can each do individually to help make change happen.

"Our ability and curiosity to learn is directly proportional to our ability to create a culture where everybody is respected, and we think of diversity as more than just a social norm, but a competitive advantage."

━━━━━ *The Honorable James Geurts, Performing the Duties of the Under Secretary of the United States Navy*

Demand more diverse representation within leadership teams.

Whether you are in a position of influence at work or you're a student attending college, your voice can help motivate those in charge to rethink whom they promote and put into leadership roles.

In politics, you can use your voice to vote for leaders who genuinely reflect their communities at every level of government (a topic we explore in the next chapter). On a corporate level, one forgotten element of "managing up" involves sharing a vocal perspective on who becomes a leader within an organization in the first place.

If you work at a company that uses "360-degree reviews" where employees at all levels are asked for feedback on peers and managers, consider if you are doing all you can to understand the perspectives of co-workers from marginalized backgrounds on whether they perceive they are getting equitable access to opportunities to succeed.

If you're a student setting your course selections for the semester, ask yourself if you are picking electives that depart from a Euro-centric perspective and consider adding courses led by instructors of color who might be given more opportunities within the institution as a result of your interest and support.

You don't need to have a fancy job title or even actually be in the workforce to help encourage and advocate for more diversity in leadership. We all have a role to play in creating a world with more inclusive leaders.

——— **ACTION #2** ———

Become an internal champion for third-party certifications and industry best practices.

Dozens of DEI certifications, advocacy programs, and industry-leading best practices exist to help any team build a more equitable workplace. Any of these could benefit your organization, but in most cases there needs to be an internal advocate who manages the process. What would it take for *you* to become that champion?

Choosing to lead an internal initiative not only creates change from the bottom up but also provides an excellent opportunity to build your own career and solidify your reputation as someone who believes that more inclusive leadership matters.

Coming from a marginalized background is not a necessary qualification for getting involved. Anyone who truly believes in the importance of representation and cultures of belonging can take the first step toward engaging with these third-party groups.

Recognize your bias in how you speak about leaders or portray them through imagery.

The stock image of a boardroom filled with men is easy to find online. Similarly, there are plenty of traditional images of leadership, from older men standing behind podiums to White hands shaking to seal a deal. Many of us have near-daily opportunities to make choices that perpetuate these same stereotypes—or challenge them.

Can you choose a stock image that shows a different type of leader at the front of the room? Will you call out those documents or people who regularly refer to a CEO, doctor, or boss as "him"?

These may seem like small actions, but rethinking the way we approach them helps us create a more inclusive perception of who a leader can and "should" be, as well as retrain ourselves in our own unexamined biases. The more we adjust the visuals and language around leadership now, the more likely it is for young people of all identities to grow up in a world where they can see themselves reflected among the many types of leaders they see around them.

Beyond Diversity In
LEADERSHIP

🏛 WHAT NEEDS TO HAPPEN:

- ❯ The "glass ceiling" cannot be replaced with the "glass cliff."
- ❯ Mentorship must be available to all, not only a select few.
- ❯ Diverse leadership cannot be treated as a "one and done" challenge.

WHAT *YOU* CAN DO:

- ❯ Demand more diverse representation within leadership teams.
- ❯ Become an internal champion for third-party certifications and industry best practices.
- ❯ Recognize your bias in how you speak about leaders or portray them through imagery.

💬 CONVERSATION STARTERS:

- ❯ Consider your personal leadership style: do you emphasize inclusion or vulnerability as a key quality? Why or why not?
- ❯ Think of a time you had an effective mentor. What did they do to make you feel included or heard? How can you do the same for someone else?

BEYOND DIVERSITY IN
GOVERNMENT

"I think change needs to be egoless. It's not about leaving my fingerprints or a legacy. It's more important to be part of a process."

— *Her Majesty Queen Rania Al Abdullah of Jordan*

Chapter Summary:

Government should be representative of people, but there is often a persistent experience gap between elected officials and the communities they are meant to represent. Building a more inclusive society requires us to remove barriers to voting, elect candidates who truly represent their constituents and support the grassroots advocacy organizations working to create collective impact.

How It Is...

"I've never been an activist or really involved in politics at all," says Jackie Huba. As a published author and expert in marketing, Jackie's path never intersected with political organizing. But that changed after the United States presidential election of 2016.

Upon learning that 100 *million* people did not vote that year,[1] and that one in five LGBTQ+ people was not even registered to vote,[2] Jackie imagined an unusual way to improve voter turnout.

"I thought, what if we could mobilize the biggest movement of drag artists in the country on a national scale to register people and get them out to vote?" Having an active presence in the drag community herself, Jackie began leveraging her connections to build a nationwide coalition of queer artists and voting rights advocates.

In 2019, Drag Out The Vote™ was formally established as a nonpartisan, nonprofit organization that works with drag performers to promote civic participation. The connection of drag artists to political movements has a long history. Drag artists—from Stonewall to the Sisters of Perpetual Indulgence—have been active in social movements for decades. For the 2020 US presidential election, Drag Out The Vote recruited 300 drag artists in 44 states to successfully get thousands of people voting in their communities.

The Disability Visibility Project, founded by disabled activist Alice Wong, is another notable example. The organization started the

#CripTheVote campaign to advocate not only for more accessible voting processes, but also to support more disabled candidates.

There are currently hundreds of grassroots organizing efforts like these which have successfully integrated more voices into democratic processes across the world. Those efforts engage voters based on their passions, their ethnicity, the regions where they live, and their religious beliefs. Aside from community organizations, some countries are also introducing formal legislation aimed at opening the democratic process to groups who previously lacked representation, such as younger voters and women.

Following the early lead of countries like Brazil and Nicaragua, in 2007 Austria became the first nation in the European Union to lower the voting age to 16. In 27 countries worldwide, including Belgium and the Fiji Islands, voting is required, and nonvoters can be fined. Less than a decade ago, women in Saudi Arabia were granted the right to vote after a long campaign demanding suffrage for current and future generations.

At the same time, there has been a disturbing rise in many countries of organized efforts to make voting *harder* for marginalized individuals, aiming to reduce their participation in elections. The structure of politics and government in this decade will be shaped by fundamental battles between those who want government to be more inclusive and those who want to restrict access to people who do not look and think like them.

The fight to have more marginalized voices participating in a democracy by casting their votes is only half of the battle. There must be more diverse elected and appointed officials working *inside* governments, enacting changes and speaking for those who remain invisible when policies and legislation are being shaped, debated, and passed. In this respect, many governments around the world have an even harder challenge.

In 79 of the 100 largest US cities, the percentage of White people in office exceeds the percentage of White people in the population.[3] And for queer people, the gap is even wider: openly LGBTQ+ people are at least 4.5 percent of the US adult population but hold just 0.17 percent of elected positions nationwide.[4] In addition, US citizens in regions such as Washington, DC, American Samoa, and Puerto Rico continue to lack full and accurate representation in government.

While the 2020 election cycle brought record numbers of women and people of color into the US House of Representatives, a POLITICO analysis found that "nearly every state was failing to achieve racial and gender parity with their own population data" in the lower level of the state legislatures.[5] This same issue affects governments around the world as well.

Southeast Asia represents one of the most diverse regions in the world, with more than 100 different ethnic groups speaking thousands of different languages and dialects. Yet in many of these places, a nationalist government aligned with a particular religion or ethnicity actively discriminates against those in the minority.

Even in Canada—long seen as a model for an inclusive, diverse society with leader Justin Trudeau promising and making progress "to build a government that looks like Canada"—the number of senior civil servants who are not White or male remains stubbornly below 10 percent.[6]

The bottom line is clear: too many governments around the world simply do not reflect the expanding diversity or the existing demographic reality of their people. Jyoti Sarda, producer of the documentary film *And She Could Be Next*, points out the obvious paradox inside this crisis of inclusion: "Isn't the point of government to represent? How can you represent if you don't include all voices?"

"If an organization is not achieving its diversity objectives, it's often by design. Solving the problem needs a new design built with the outcome in mind."

Michael Akinyele, Former Founding CINO at the US Department of Veterans Affairs

Governments have immense potential when it comes to building a more diverse and inclusive society, whether through necessary policy shifts like granting women the right to vote or the implementation of landmark legislation protecting the LGBTQ+ community and those with disabilities from discrimination. At the same time, governments can also be barriers to progress by keeping inequities in place to maintain the status quo.

How can governments and people avoid reverting to biased systems and beliefs, and fight back against those who wish for elected officials and policies that make our society less inclusive?

How Things Are Changing . . .

We think it's safe to say that most governments, regardless of region, have a well-earned reputation for moving slowly.

Bureaucracies exist in large companies, too, but they seem to be a consistent fixture of government. Just because a system is deeply entrenched, however, doesn't mean it can't be changed. As marketing executive and Latina business advocate Kety Esquivel shared at our summit, "Change is not going to happen overnight, and it's not going to happen with just a couple of individuals trying to create it."

58% of Americans believe that increased diversity makes their country a better place.

Source: Pew Research

In the political arena, real shifts are happening thanks to grassroots movements. We saw the recent effects of one such movement around legalizing same-sex unions in the United States. Within a few short years, the issue went from a divisive partisan sticking point to a legal reality backed by bi-partisan support.

As this example illustrates, initiatives to change popular opinion and legislation can and do succeed when bolstered by the right groundswell of public support—but it can take years of dedication and sacrifice from brave individuals to get there. The same thing is true when you consider how unlikely leaders from marginalized backgrounds come to power. When they do, they often have a big impact.

Numerous studies analyzing national responses to the COVID-19 pandemic in 2020 concluded that countries with heads of state who were women fared better during the crisis.[7] Compared to the United Kingdom, France, Italy, and Spain, as of our date of publication, the Angela Merkel-led Germany has had a far lower death rate.

Tsai Ing-wen, the president of Taiwan, steered one of the most successful efforts to contain the virus, using testing, contact tracing, and isolation measures to control infections without resorting to a complete national lockdown. New Zealand Prime Minister Jacinda Ardern made headlines when she announced on May 11, 2020, that the entire country met its ambitious goal of not only curbing but eradicating the COVID-19 virus.

Most political experts caution against attributing these results solely to the gender of the leaders behind them, but the prevalence of female leaders thriving in government does stand out as a not-so-coincidental reminder of the tangible value that comes from welcoming non-traditional voices into government. Research from the Council on Foreign Relations' Women Power Index supports this conclusion, finding that women's leadership often promotes bipartisanship, equality, and stability.[8]

A similar effect may result from including people of color and other underrepresented groups as well. In early 2021, Deb Haaland made history when she became the first Native American to serve in a cabinet secretary role within the United States, and she has since focused on sharing untold stories of Indigenous people in order to advocate on their behalf.

Jordon Steele-John, Australia's youngest federal politician at 25 years old, was born with cerebral palsy. After his election in 2017, the Australian Senate chambers were made wheelchair-accessible for the first time. New Zealand recently appointed the most diverse cabinet in the country's history with eight women, five Māori, three Pasifika, and three LGBTQ+ members serving in 2020.[9] All these are singular but nonetheless important indicators of progress.

On the other side of the political equation, we are also seeing encouraging progress in the realm of increased civic engagement. The work of American politician, lawyer, voting rights activist, and author Stacey Abrams is one example.

Abrams skyrocketed to national prominence in 2020, when she gained widespread recognition for her partnership with a coalition of Black, female elected officials and community organizers, who together built a network of organizations that highlighted voter suppression and inspired an estimated 800,000 new voters to register in Georgia.

Data from the International Institute for Democracy and Electoral Assistance (IDEA) shows that these efforts are more important than ever. Their research revealed that globally, the average voter turnout has decreased dramatically since the early 1990s.[10] Another report from Pew Research surveyed people in 14 countries and concluded that, even in places where voter turnout was above average, other forms of political participation were extremely low.[11]

Adding to the ongoing challenge of bringing more diverse perspectives into the halls of government is the fact that success stories like Abrams' efforts in Georgia repeatedly face a serious backlash, whether through fearmongering legislation, social intimidation, or other efforts aimed at making voter participation more difficult for marginalized groups.

What Needs To Happen . . .

The question we are left with is how will we meet this twofold challenge to increase diversity among elected officials *and* make participation in government more inclusive as well? What will it take for underrepresented populations to participate in democratic processes at a greater rate and to ensure their voices are heard? And how can candidates and elected officials better represent the communities they come from?

Moving forward, conquering resistance from a political establishment unwilling to share power will require collective effort that inspires change and increases diversity in government. Here are some concrete steps we must take to move us closer to this goal.

IMPERATIVE #1

Bring attention to local elections and support new voices running against incumbent candidates.

Every four years, a massive wave of marketing campaigns encourage eligible citizens to vote in the US presidential election. State and local elections held in the years between receive far less attention.

In any democracy, many decisions are shaped at the local level. This is where inequity starts, and when you have unqualified or biased individuals winning, it severely impacts the overall equity of government.

When prejudiced or ethically compromised people take office, their actions institutionalize their biases. It is a quantifiable fact that, globally speaking, incumbent candidates tend to fare better among underinformed voters—many of whom simply cast a ballot for the candidate they are already familiar with.[12]

Electing unknown leaders that better represent the diversity of their constituents begins with the casting of informed ballots at a local level. That remains harder to achieve than it should be.

How can we break people out of their complacency and make it easier for them to get informed and participate in the democratic process? It starts with awareness, constant reminders, and a consistent message that underscores just how much these smaller and more frequent local elections matter. People will only participate when it feels critically important to do so.

IMPERATIVE #2

Make voting more accessible by removing barriers and exposing those who try to prevent participation.

Pervasive voter suppression remains one of the biggest challenges to advancing diverse voices in government and achieving fairness and equity in society.

Local lawmakers need to break down policies that uphold voter suppression, ranging from felony disenfranchisement to strict voter ID requirements, and work to end gerrymandering—the practice of manipulating regional voting boundaries to favor one political party over another.

Targeted policies like these already lead to vastly disparate voting experiences between different demographics. For example, one study in the US found that Black voters wait 45 minutes longer to vote in person—and Latinx voters wait 46 minutes longer—than the average White voter.[13] Many polling places around the world are also inaccessible to those with a physical disability, excluding another large group from being able to easily participate. Recently, the efforts to make voting harder have gotten even more intense.

Solving this issue means supporting and amplifying the work of advocacy organizations dedicated to combating issues such as voter suppression or intimidation. It can mean working to get more people registered to vote. It also means providing on-the-ground resources (or supporting the organizations who do) to make these things happen, which can mean hiring language translation services, transporting citizens to polling places, and publishing constant proactive reminders and prompts that encourage people to follow through and vote. [14]

 Download our list of advocacy groups at www.nonobviousdiversity.com/resources

IMPERATIVE #3

Institutions need to reckon with past injustices, discrimination, and governmental bias.

Sometimes moving *forward* requires looking *backward*. Institutions also need to hold themselves accountable and increase their awareness of how government agencies, systems, and leaders have enacted harm toward marginalized populations in the near and distant past.

As India Thusi, associate professor of law at the Delaware Law School noted at our summit, "There has been a broad acknowledgment that institutions play a role in perpetuating racial injustice, and many institutions have been openly engaging with and reflecting about this."

Reckoning with our historical reality—whether by reading about it, discussing it with peers and friends, showing up to related protests, or by actually making monetary reparations—is an important first step toward creating a better future.

Addressing past injustices can be uncomfortable but necessary: it sends the important message that underrepresented groups will no longer be ignored or marginalized by their government. This is not about creating victims or assigning blame for past actions to modern generations. Rather it is a chance to build a shared understanding of what happened and, most importantly, it represents a shared consensus that we must never let it happen again.

What You Can Do . . .

Though it sounds cliché in the context of drastic political polarization, government is indeed one of the few places in our societies where each of us has the opportunity to unite, express a shared voice, and shape the society we choose to live in.

The insights from panelists at our summit helped us compile some personal actions each of us could take to influence government to be more inclusive no matter where we live.

Confront and converse with differing opinions.

In an increasingly polarized world, it's becoming commonplace to dismiss and discount differing beliefs without giving them a second thought. Political and business talk show host Angela Ward warns, "If we can't communicate properly, there's no way we can sit and listen to each other or understand each other's point." We must welcome human nuance and gray areas into our political discussions, and to do this, all of us need to grow more comfortable with discursive conflict and political dissonance.

The only way we can accomplish this as individuals is by suspending our judgment and choosing to listen and engage with others, instead of dismissing and silencing them. Daryl Davis is perhaps the best example of someone who has made a lifetime habit out of having these types of conversations.

For decades now, he has dedicated himself to changing the minds of an unlikely group: members of the Klu Klux Klan. As a Black musician now in his 60s, Davis represents an unusual perspective in the global fight against racism. His "weapon" of choice is an old-fashioned, face-to-face conversation.

Davis estimates he has influenced more than 200 former White supremacists to change their views. It is the stunning outcome of a lifetime of work from one man, especially when you consider how many *others* those 200 people might have gone on to influence after they gave up their White robes. It is also an example that all of us can learn from.

"If I can sit down and talk to K.K.K. members and neo-Nazis . . . there's no reason why somebody can't sit down at a dinner table and talk to their family member."[15]

Daryl Davis, Musician and Anti-Racism Advocate

When we engage in difficult human conversations, we can shift people's views in a positive way—and this translates directly into politics through the candidates they support and the policies they demand.

ACTION #2

Get involved with community partners and grassroots groups.

As African American writer, feminist, and civil rights advocate Audre Lorde famously said, "The master's tools will never dismantle the master's house." To address the issue of dismantling dominant and discriminatory political systems, we all must support the local and regional collaborations that are working to create *collective impact*.

The term describes how the efforts of multiple groups working on a related issue can multiply their effectiveness if supported altogether.

The most impactful grassroots efforts are often the ones most focused on building coalitions, collaborating with related groups and prioritizing actions that bring people together instead of fighting alone.

——— **ACTION #3** ———

Act with purposeful urgency.

Given the dense bureaucracy of government and the long-winded nature of election cycles, it's easy to get discouraged by slow progress. Regardless of the time it takes, we all must remember that acting with purpose is the only way to build momentum toward equity objectives. If you have a message you want to get out there, share it with persistence and passion. If there is an organization doing work that you deeply believe in, support and amplify their efforts even during years when there is no presidential election cycle.

Most importantly, ask yourself: what is the most effective way to be heard in your community? Is it direct canvassing, online petitions and email correspondence, public demonstrations, social media campaigns, holding town halls, or making artwork?

The more involved and invested you are, the more you can inspire a similar level of engagement from others in your community. Active participation, like apathy, can be contagious. Choose to be active.

Beyond Diversity In
GOVERNMENT

🏛 WHAT NEEDS TO HAPPEN:

- ❯ Bring attention to local elections and support new voices running against incumbent candidates.

- ❯ Make voting more accessible by removing barriers and exposing those who try to prevent participation.

- ❯ Institutions need to reckon with past injustices, discrimination, and governmental bias.

WHAT *YOU* CAN DO:

- ❯ Confront and converse with differing opinions.

- ❯ Get involved with community partners and grassroots groups.

- ❯ Act with purposeful urgency.

💬 CONVERSATION STARTERS:

- ❯ What political figures personally give you hope, and why?

- ❯ In your local community, who is—and perhaps more importantly, who isn't—currently involved?

BEYOND DIVERSITY IN
THE FUTURE

"Look closely at the present you are constructing: it should look like the future you are dreaming."

— Alice Walker, Author and Pulitzer Prize Winner

Chapter Summary:

In the past, the decisions about where and how we will live, who will have access to resources and the way we treat the environment have routinely excluded marginalized voices. As a result we live in cities and towns built decades ago based on long-standing biases and disparities. Creating a more equitable future must involve the voices of people from all communities and build upon their input.

How It Is . . .

People love to imagine the future. The ones who do it professionally are known as *futurists*.

For years the prototypical "futurist" that you might find speaking on the biggest stages and consulting for the world's most forward-thinking companies or nations was typically older, White, male, abled, and European (or maybe North American).

While the World Future Society recently estimated that just over 20 percent of their members are women[1] and that the field has been getting more diverse overall—people of color and women remain dramatically underrepresented among futurists. This is a reality that Rohit understands first-hand having worked as an Indian American "reluctant futurist" for the past decade.

The idea of being called a futurist always felt limiting to him. Futurists typically write and talk about the long-term, optimistic future. They imagine jet packs, evolved societies, and utopias. Often these ideas—which sometimes blur the line between fiction and reality—can serve to obscure the real impact futurism has on the world of *today*.

In the past decade of writing and publishing his Non-Obvious Trend book series, and eventually his *Non-Obvious Megatrends*, Rohit has focused on curating and anticipating the *near future*. Efforts like these don't just *predict* the future, they help us to *imagine* it as well. And for too long, the most popular predictions have lacked the broader perspective.

"The one reason why futurism as a discipline is so White and male, is because White males have the ability to offer the most optimistic vision. They can get up on stage and tell us that the world will be okay, that technology will fix all our problems, that we'll live forever."

Madeline Ashby, Science Fiction Writer and Futurist

Until recently, conversations about how we are going to build our future society—where and how we will live, who will have access to technology and what kind of environment we will leave future generations—have routinely ignored underrepresented groups. We live in cities and towns that were built decades (and even centuries) ago based on deeply rooted biases that are still alive today, and which were reinforced in physical ways through choices made by past leaders. These cities and towns were often designed to *intentionally* keep groups segregated—and that segregation has led to further inequities.

For example, during the 1930s, the US government sponsored the creation of color-coded lending maps that marked areas populated by largely Black American residents in bright, red ink. This practice, eventually termed "redlining," used the color as a warning that these residents were deemed risky and unworthy of investment. Other particularly brazen examples are the notorious efforts of urban planner Robert Moses, who intentionally built highways through the middle of minority neighborhoods and designed bridges low enough to prevent city buses—likely carrying poor minorities—from passing underneath to reach higher income areas such as beachfront properties.

By 2050, about 70% of the world's population is expected to live in urban areas.

Source: United Nations

The development of technology and the infrastructure built from biased maps have also contributed to this inequity. Consider the internet—arguably the one innovation from the past two decades that has most changed how we live, work, learn, and connect with others.

While engineers were building the infrastructure that supports our current access to the internet, decisions about where to extend its service were often based on economic agendas. Unsurprisingly, that almost always left the poorest, most marginalized communities as the least connected. Not having access to the internet—a near-necessity in today's world—has only served to reinforce the deep divisions and lack of access that already existed along these socioeconomic lines.

The choices that were made in the past about the environment have also had a similarly detrimental effect on our planet, contributing to the wealth of the few and creating a planet facing dangerous climate change. These effects have hit underrepresented minorities and undeveloped countries harder than other groups.

Across each of these areas, we can see how the choices of past generations have shaped the inequities that exist in our world today. So what can we do to ensure that the choices we make now lay a foundation for a society that is more diverse and inclusive for future generations?

"Scholars have often cast the census as an instrument of power . . . but the census can be a tool, too, of the powerless. It has been embraced, appropriated, and even subverted by those being counted. It has served as a medium for individual and minority self-expression."

Andrew Whitby, *Author of The Sum of the People*

Many of these choices are being made right now. Government census efforts are being used to shape public policy for the future. Automation is playing an increasingly central role in our lives. Medical advancements are extending our lifespans—and by extension our working years as well.

All of this rapid change is fueling big questions about the future. In a world where workers can be displaced by technology, how will inequity affect who loses the first jobs? How will the escalating effects of climate change and environmental concerns affect the way we work and live? Finally, on a societal level, will the already widening cultural and technological chasm between people of different backgrounds and geographies continue to deepen, or will we manage to find new ways to bridge the gap?

Creators of fiction have long imagined future scenarios that are either hopeful utopias or cautionary dystopias. Across literature and entertainment, it seems the dystopias are currently more popular—perhaps revealing our human desire to imagine the worst to feel better about our own reality by comparison.

Here we take inspiration from the futurists of the past and present to imagine a more inclusive future.

How Things Are Changing . . .

More than a decade ago, the World Health Organization launched the WHO Global Network for Age-friendly Cities and Communities. The project was intended to share ideas for making communities more accessible. More than 800 mayors in 40 countries joined the movement. Their results have been inspiring.

In Ottawa, Canada, neighborhood walking audits resulted in the passage of a new speed reduction policy, audible pedestrian signals, and improved signage. In Porto, Portugal, local government facilitated a program that matches senior citizens willing to share their homes with younger students seeking lodging, thus combating older adults' reports of social isolation while simultaneously fostering intergenerational connections.

"It's really important that all government agencies are engaging people with disabilities in a meaningful way, not as an afterthought. If you figure out how to turn on the electricity—disability access needs to be another line item in the budget."

■■■■■■■■■■■■■■■■■ *Janice Lintz, Hearing Access Consultant & Advocate*

Aside from making our physical spaces more accessible, there are many also working on addressing the so-called "digital divide"—the gap between those who have ready access to the internet and those who don't. In the US, members of the Rural Broadband Association (NTCA) are collaborating to bring high-speed internet to otherwise unserved communities, and to run inclusive training and certification programs to help these communities build the skills to not only install the technology, but also to maintain and support it themselves over the long term.

This idea of involving the local community in the imagining and building of the future is at the heart of the work that Hajj Flemings is leading as well. As the founder of an organization called Rebrand Cities, Flemings is working to get diverse small businesses internet access and has the ambitious goal of putting 10,000 underrepresented small businesses online, thus using technology as an equalizer and gateway to the new world of opportunities and revenue.

Turning to environmental issues, the movement is also starting to involve the underrepresented voices of those most deeply impacted by the effects of pollution and carbon emissions.

Throughout the past few decades, the activists who were widely known or featured in media, documentaries, and magazine articles tended to be older, White, and from a developed Western nation. Jacques Cousteau, Jane Goodall, and Sir David Attenborough are all classic examples.

These legends were icons for subsequent generations of environmental activists. Today, the prototype of the environmental activist is shifting. The efforts of women like Yale's Professor of Environmental Justice, Dr. Dorceta E. Taylor, or 19-year old Mexican-Indigenous climate justice activist Xiye Bastida, are gaining more recognition.

Their work, by necessity, must also focus on a different element of the battle against climate change. Dr. Taylor, for example, has written often about environmental racism and "how conservation ideas and politics are tied to social dynamics such as racism, classism, and gender discrimination."[2]

Bastida has often been called the "Greta Thunberg of America," a reference to the widely known young Swedish climate activist who challenged world leaders to take immediate action and inspired a generation of students to get involved. The comparison itself illustrates both the progress being made and how far we have to go. In Bastida's words, "Just because we have the same mission, it doesn't mean that we have the same struggles, inspirations, criticisms, or stories."[3]

To truly tackle the future challenge of climate change, marginalized voices like these must continue to be celebrated, shared, and invited to participate more directly in the conversations about the issues they are passionate about.

"The White response to climate change is literally suffocating to people of color. Climate anxiety can operate like White fragility, sucking up all the oxygen in the room and devoting resources toward appeasing the dominant group."

Sarah Jaquette Ray, PhD and Author of
A Field Guide to Climate Anxiety

Urban planning has also lacked diverse voices in the past. Urban policy expert and professor of psychiatry Dr. Mindy Thompson Fullilove describes this as our "ecology of inequality." To illustrate, she shares the cautionary tale of the Delmar Divide—a name given to the dividing line running east to west along Delmar Boulevard in St. Louis, which has long served as a sort of racial and socioeconomic segregation line throughout the city.

Even decades later, residents living north of the dividing line are estimated to be 98 percent Black and continue to experience "hypervacancy"—a term used to describe a region where the housing market has essentially stopped growing.[4]

This type of geographic segregation can be the starting point for many other inequities. It can lead to what food justice activist Karen Washington and others describe as "food apartheid"—a more powerful term than "food desert"—which encapsulates the situation faced by many people living in urban areas and lacking access to a grocery store or healthier food alternatives, because larger retailers don't see those locations as profitable. The economic prosperity, and lack thereof, over a distance as minimal as two city blocks is a stark reminder that despite our advances, we still have a very long way to go.

Across futurist conversations, technology initiatives, urban planning projects, infrastructure development, or environmental advocacy, it can't solely be the wealthy and privileged who make the decisions that impact future economic prosperity for some— and result in economic depression for so many others.

"The future can only be healthier, fairer, and greener if we listen to voices who are most involved in shaping it."

▬▬▬▬▬▬ **Henry Coutinho-Mason, Co-author of The Future Normal**

Planning for a more equitable and fair future for everyone requires us to include, elevate, and respond to the voices of people from all communities—and to shape the future based on what all people actually need.

What Needs To Happen . . .

As we think about how our world could be, the questions we ask (and who has the chance to ask them) will shape what actions we need to take *today* to make that foundation as inclusive as it can be for tomorrow.

IMPERATIVE #1

Prioritize marginalized voices in the conversations and decisions about urban and future planning.

In her book *Invisible Women*, author Caroline Criado Perez exposes how our modern world has been largely built *by* men and *for* men. Correcting this entrenched mindset must start by making urban planning teams—and particularly their leadership—more diverse and inclusive. There are some hopeful signs that this may soon happen. Despite the fact that just 10 percent of the highest-ranking jobs at leading architecture firms and urban planning offices are held by women, more than half of recent urban planning graduates were women, indicating a generational shift may be on its way.[5]

When women *do* get involved, and their needs and ideas are respected, the impact can be significant.

The city of Vienna in Austria became one of the first places to test this theory when city administrators began to "create laws, rules, and regulations that benefit men and women equally" back in the 1990s.[6] Known as "Gender Mainstreaming," the public policy effort has had a significant impact on the design of public transportation systems in the Austrian capital ever since, and their progress has inspired similar initiatives across the world.

"We must increase female representation in all spheres of life. Because as more women move into positions of power or influence, there's another pattern that is becoming even more apparent: women simply don't forget that women exist as easily as men often seem to."

Caroline Criado Perez, Author of Invisible Women

According to data from the World Resources Institute (WRI), between 50 percent to 80 percent of all urban employment is made up of "informal workers"[7]—a term used to describe everything from street vendors to rickshaw pullers. The voices of these workers are also routinely left out of any urban planning decisions. In South Africa, an organization called Asiye eTafuleni (AeT) has been working to change this since 2008.

AeT's efforts to work with informal vendors, developers, and the government, to save more than 3,000 jobs by preventing the historic Warwick Junction central market in Durban from being redeveloped into a shopping mall, received widespread recognition across the world.[8]

Together these examples illustrate a clear conclusion. When urban planning gets more inclusive, so does our collective future.

Bridge the digital divide by using technology as a proactive tool for equity and inclusion.

Broadband internet is not a universally accessible utility in most places throughout the world, and an increasing number of policy experts, technologists, and everyday people are working to change this. The communities least likely to have broadband access tend to be those in depressed socioeconomic areas and rural locations. One solution experts have identified for this accessibility problem is increasing government subsidies to provide internet access, coupled with the enactment of legislation that redefines what qualifies as "broadband" so quality of access can be tracked accurately.

43% of adults with lower incomes do not have home broadband internet services.

Source: Pew Research

As policy expert Gigi Sohn noted during our summit, "The maps that purport to show who has broadband and who doesn't are grossly inaccurate, and significantly overstate who has access to high-speed internet." In addition, the companies who hold spectrum licenses to provide broadband coverage in many less populous rural areas (especially tribal lands) might fail to build networks in those areas. These are challenges that can be addressed through smart policy changes and influenced by more public engagement and conversation.

IMPERATIVE #3

Overhaul or replace systems put in place in the past that continue to create systemic inequality today.

Stories like the Delmar Divide are common in communities across the world. Sometimes they are the result of decades-old political choices like neighborhood zoning laws. In other cases, they are the result of economic incentives that make it more lucrative to use open land for a parking garage, instead of a community center.

"Government action, not the generosity of the global elite, is the best solution to some of our most deep-seated problems."

Anand Giridharadas, Author of Winners Take All

We need to break the cycle. Governments must identify and correct policies that unfairly discriminate against entire communities and prioritize profit over people. Corporations and investors must also examine their own roles in keeping these inequities in place. Only through widespread recognition of these choices will we be able to imagine a more inclusive future.

What *You* Can Do . . .

The future can feel like a vague societal concept shaped by the institutions and leaders around us instead of something that we have the ability to impact. The truth is, there are many ways that our personal actions can help to shape the near and long-term future of the places that we live in. Let's look at three in particular.

ACTION #1

Listen and learn from the perspectives of people from generations other than your own.

The late comedian George Carlin was fond of joking that, "Anybody driving slower than you is an idiot, and anyone going faster than you is a maniac." The same mindset might also explain why most people tend to minimize the voices of those from generations other than their own.

In order to build a more inclusive future, each of us must confront our own biases in how we treat those who are either older or younger than ourselves.

Are you dismissing the opinion and counsel of a colleague older than you as outdated or old-fashioned? Are you minimizing a perspective or social movement simply because it is mainly propelled by people younger than you?

"One thing is for certain, the more profoundly baffled you have been in your life, the more open your mind becomes to new ideas."

Neil deGrasse Tyson, American Scientist

We each have moments in our professional and personal lives when we can choose to show mutual respect and open-mindedness toward people who are generationally different. One specific way we can all do this is by seeking out a personal mentor. While the idea of having an older professional mentor is widely understood and supported, the idea of a *reverse* mentor remains somewhat niche. Both have great value once we realize that we all have the capacity to learn from those who are both older *and* younger than ourselves.

ACTION #2

Join the fight to make future technology more inclusive, less biased and more widely accessible.

Across many chapters of this book, we've seen examples of organizations fighting against bias and using technology as a force for more equity. There are a wide range of groups using technology and access to it as a way to break down systemic biases and create a more diverse and inclusive world.

Yet bias in technology through algorithms poses many risks to systematize discrimination. The only way we can all ensure that the technology being developed and implemented in the future makes our world more inclusive is by actively demanding that it is designed that way and made available to everyone regardless of ability, race, gender, or geographic location.

ACTION #3

Learn from and share the pioneering work of underrepresented voices in futurism.

We opened this chapter with a story of how the insular world of futurists has long been associated with thinkers from a single perspective. Today, this once narrow field is experiencing an influx of alternate viewpoints that are described through an ever-widening range of research specialties such as Afrofuturism, Queer Futurism, Gulf Futurism, Neo-Futurism, Indigenous Futurism, Chicanafuturism, and many others.

"Futurists ask what tomorrow's hoverboards and flying cars are made of. Afrofuturists ask: who will build them?"[9]

C. Brandon Ogbunu, Assistant Professor, Yale University

What each term represents is an entirely unique way of writing, researching, and imagining the future through a different lens. Have you heard any of these terms before? Whether you answered yes or no, you have a chance to educate yourself more deeply about any of these viewpoints by starting to read their proponents' insights and ideas.

Each of them offers a starting point for imagining alternate futures from a variety of perspectives. The importance of this cannot be overstated. The more we can individually challenge our assumptions about the future, the more we can see alternate and more inclusive futures for all people—futures that can then be transformed into reality.

Beyond Diversity In
THE FUTURE

🏛 WHAT NEEDS TO HAPPEN:

- ❯ Prioritize marginalized voices in the conversations and decisions about urban and future planning.

- ❯ Bridge the digital divide by using technology as a proactive tool for equity and inclusion.

- ❯ Overhaul or replace systems put in place in the past that continue to create systemic inequality today.

WHAT *YOU* CAN DO:

- ❯ Listen and learn from the perspectives of people from generations other than your own.

- ❯ Join the fight to make future technology more inclusive, less biased and more widely accessible.

- ❯ Learn from and share the pioneering work of underrepresented voices in futurism.

💬 CONVERSATION STARTERS:

- ❯ How has your community, town, or city evolved in the time you've spent in it and do you feel it has become more or less inclusive?

- ❯ What are some ways that the structures and spaces around you might create inequity?

CONCLUSION

> "A gathering is a moment of time that has the potential to alter many other moments of time. And for it to have the best chance of doing so, engaging in some meaning-making at the end is crucial."
>
> ## — PRIYA PARKER, AUTHOR OF
> ## THE ART OF GATHERING

In the last few days leading up to the filming of sessions for the Non-Obvious Beyond Diversity Summit, our team was producing a guide for our moderators on how to conduct sessions and keep the conversation moving. At the time, there was one important question constantly on our minds: how would we make sure that the hours of conversation we had convened would actually create some *impact* in the world?

The question had been fueling an intense debate within our organizing team. Should we create some sort of charter or certification for attendees? What if we charged a ticket fee for people to attend and donated the funds to charitable organizations? And how could we hope to have a real dialogue when most of our anticipated audience would be watching the event on-demand in the months (or even years) after the summit was over?

Writing this book was the longer-term answer, but in that moment we made a decision that fueled the entire mission and tone of the event. We required every one of our moderators to end each session by asking panelists for *immediately* actionable guidance. If we were going to go beyond conversation, we decided that it was important to ask some hard questions and get some concrete advice.

In our daily lives, it's easy to feel disoriented after a powerful experience.

We can listen to transformative keynote speakers at events and get inspired. Then we get back to the office, unsure of what to change in our own lives. We can watch groundbreaking documentaries that convince us of the importance of making healthier or more environmentally friendly choices, and soon after we go back to our same typical habits.

Changing ourselves and our actions is hard.

In her book *The Art of Gathering*, author Priya Parker frames the duty to create lasting impact after a gathering as a challenge of "reentry." The term is used in many situations to describe the task of "helping someone who has gone through an intense experience within the bubble of dialogue return to their original context."

After reading this book and watching the videos from our summit, you are going to return to your daily life. This might mean heading back to class, leading a team at work or going back to running your own business. Regardless of the world you're returning to, the task of shaping your own reentry is one you are about to face.

Early in the book we wrote about the idea of intersectionality as a way that each of us might define and embrace our unique identities. As we explored many different perspectives, we tried to use them to inspire more chances for intersectional thinking as well. It may have started with a conversation, but the ultimate goal is to help you create more opportunities to practice this type of thinking with every interaction you have.

An inclusive world starts with each of us choosing to respect perspectives other than our own, treating everyone with respect and choosing to stand up for others who need our support. More than anything else, this is what going *beyond diversity* truly means.

ACKNOWLEDGMENTS

"There is no power for change greater than a community discovering what it cares about."

**— MARGARET J. WHEATLEY,
AMERICAN WRITER AND PROFESSOR**

People are generous.

We learned many things from the journey to write *Beyond Diversity*, but this was the most energizing. When you ask people to give their time, passion, and expertise to something worthwhile … they show up. This book exists because of the number of people who said yes when asked to tell their stories.

So to start we must offer our heartfelt gratitude for the trust they have put in us to share their lived experience and wisdom with you. In addition to the voices you might have watched in sessions from the summit or the perspectives you read throughout the book, there was also a vibrant community of creators who helped in the development of both our summit and this book.

On the editorial side, in addition to our stellar list of contributors including Andrius Alvarez-Backus, Chhavi Arya, Karen Dahms, Sandhya Jain-Patel, Kaleena Sales and Monika Samtani, we want to thank our extended editorial team of Genoveva Llosa, Kameron Bryant-Sergejev, and Emily Montague for their tireless efforts to make every aspect of this book better.

The design of the cover was inspired by the mosaic artwork of Zharia Shinn, which fit perfectly with the actionable theme of the book and the challenge for all of us to "Be It." The full cover and interior came to life through the collaborative efforts of Amanda Hudson, Paul Nielsen and the Faceout Studios team along with the tireless efforts of Jessica Angerstein to get every detail right.

A book like this requires a diversity of perspectives as well, and we were lucky to have an amazing team of sensitivity readers who helped us to ensure the language, examples and tone throughout the book were as inclusive as possible. A big thanks to our entire team of readers, including Kenrya Rankin, Jen O'Ryan, Sarosh Arif, Zhui Ning Chang, Alexandrea Gill, Anna Everts, Aubrey Kobayashi, Noemi Martinez, W. Muruli, Zarmina Rafi, Anaya Walker, and Allison Wallis.

The summit that first inspired this book also engaged a small army of producers, interns and creators to help organize the sessions, manage the details, edit and transcribe the videos and manage the ongoing community we created through the event. Our organizing team of Chhavi Arya, Rohi Mirza Pandya, Amy Kean, Marnie McMahon, Sandhya Jain-Patel, Renee Strom,

Monika Samtani, and Jacqueline Sibanda were the core team that brought the summit to life and created the experience that would eventually become this book. Thanks also to our partner organizations who contributed to the summit, including: The Fem Word, Getty Images, Syncwords, SRC-Partners, Pass the Mic Media, Six Things Impossible, DICE, Wipro, NBC, NTCA and all the "unofficial" others.

During our summit, one practice we adopted that offered a meaningful start to many of our sessions was an Indigenous Land Acknowledgment. Even for our virtual event, we wanted to offer respect to the lands that we all occupied and worked with several of our panelists to craft a good statement. In this section, we not only wanted to give the same thanks, but also share the text that we developed in case it is helpful for you to use at your own virtual or live events:

> *Before we begin, I'd like to take a moment and reflect upon the history of the Indigenous lands we call home. While we are meeting today on a virtual platform, all of us occupy spaces that carry the powerful legacy of these diverse peoples and their unique local cultures. Through this acknowledgment, we reaffirm a deep commitment to improving our understanding of America's shared heritage, and recognize our collective responsibility to improve the bonds between all nations. We are grateful for the opportunity to meet you wherever you may be on your journey towards a more diverse and inclusive society, so that we can do the work together.*

Our summit team was also supported by Parag Mehta, Amita Vyas, Rashi Shyam, Natasha Samtani, Junish Arora, Kapil

Kapoor, Mitch Joel, Henry Coutinho-Mason, Amanda Pindus, Shubha Iyengar, Lalit Vadlamani, Hugh Forrest, Sree Sreenivasan, Neil Parikh, and Steve Taylor; as well as our amazing team of interns: Luna Abadia, Arya Bansal, Rohan Bhargava, Manav Gandhi, Krisana Goel, Eesha Madan, Maya Marathe, Meghna Parameswaran, and Diya Shyam.

This project was also enabled by the many members of the Jennifer Brown Consulting team, who every day bring us their great insights from working in the field to deliver DEI strategies, as well as their personal lived experiences. Special gratitude goes to the management, marketing, and logistics guidance of Naakai Addy, Sophie Bales, Holly Kalyn, and Rob Beaven.

It is not an exaggeration to say that more than 200 people were directly or indirectly involved in the production of this book and simply mentioning their names here in the book is the most minimal form of thanks we can offer. To do more than that, we'd like to close by sharing one final request.

The voices featured in this book and the ones who helped to create it deserve your support, recognition and partnership. If you have a chance to hire them, or buy from them, or mentor them, or engage them as *your* advisor … you should do it. A more inclusive world starts with all of us choosing to support one another.

APPENDIX:
TERMINOLOGY

Table settings tell a story. Everything from the utensils to the type of napkins used set an expectation for guests. Similarly, we wanted to take a moment to offer the same type of setting around the language, terms, and expressions you have read throughout this book.

As we shared in the first pages of this book, words matter. But this section is not meant to be a disclaimer. Instead, it is a statement of what we believe through the words we chose to use.

Our shared language can shift quickly. A decade ago, hardly anyone knew the word *selfie*. Today it's in the Merriam-Webster dictionary. By the time you read this, some of the words we use may already feel dated while others may be in the dictionary themselves (if they aren't already).

For us, the journey to write this book involved deep introspection around word choices and we want to share this candidly and transparently with you. An immediately noticeable choice we made early on was to capitalize the usage of various racial identities, including Black, Brown, Indigenous and White. One of the guideposts in that decision was to follow the lead of the National Association of Black Journalists style guide, which recommends "that whenever a color is used to appropriately describe race then it should be capitalized, including White and Brown."

Our decision to capitalize White in particular, was further informed by policy guidance framed by the Center for the Study of Social Policy which also resonated strongly with us:

> "To not name 'White' as a race is, in fact, an anti-Black act which frames Whiteness as both neutral and the standard ... We believe that it is important to call attention to White as a race as a way to understand and give voice to how Whiteness functions in our social and political institutions and our communities. Moreover, the detachment of 'White' as a proper noun allows White people to sit out of conversations about race and removes accountability from White people's and White institutions' involvement in racism."

As sociologist, author, and poet Eve Ewing so eloquently states: "When we ignore the specificity and significance of Whiteness— the things that it is, the things that it does—we contribute to its seeming neutrality and thereby grant it power to maintain its invisibility."

There is significant debate on this topic, as there is for many terms in the DEI space, and we don't expect there will be universal agreement with our choice. However, we believe by intentionally choosing to capitalize Black, Brown, Indigenous, and White, we are taking yet another small action to move towards a more fair and inclusive world.

You may also notice what appear to be inconsistencies in the book related to acronyms (LGBT, LGBTQ , LGBTQ+) or terms used to describe segments of the population (BIPOC in some places, People of Color in others, or "minorities" and "underrepresented communities" or "historically marginalized communities").

In some cases, this is due to a term used in cited materials.

Most of the identifiers we use in the book are used widely today and reflect the preferences of the different communities they represent. For maximum inclusion, we choose not to limit ourselves to the use of just one label.

Female and male, men and women are also used throughout this book. And because of a few technical glitches in the English language, these are often conflated into a biological fixed state of being. They are not. Neither are they the "either / or" determinant for humans. There are myriad ways of being (nonbinary, agender, genderfluid) and our shared understanding of this is just getting started. These "inconsistencies" also have a job. They help us see the limitations of language and our reliance on external social or cultural cues in order to make meaning.

Gender, race, ethnicity, belief systems, attractions, social roles.... we're never just one isolated event. So, we leverage what is available (words, written structures, supporting images) and hope for the best. While it can be unsettling to read through older works with outdated terms, this is an important part of the journey. Understanding how we (collectively) got here provides a framework. It also shines a light on how much more is actually possible.

 See our full list of recommended DEI glossaries at www.nonobviousdiversity.com/resources

About the Artist: Zharia Shinn

Zharia Shinn is the queen of paper collage! She works in New York while exploring the distortion of pre-existing notions of beauty and creating a new context for her psychological portraits. Her paper portraits broaden the context that surrounds the visual representation of African American women and men through an array of mediums such as, but not limited to, decorated papers and patterned fabrics. With a B.F.A. in Illustration from Rhode Island School of Design, her work has been presented internationally and domestically in group exhibitions, competitions, publications, magazines, and much more. She wholeheartedly believes that in order to see change in your environment, you have to first make the change within yourself, no matter how big or small. Don't be afraid to "be it", whether that be in your family, place of work, hometown, etc. This will then encourage others to rise to the occasion, and produce the significant change we all need on a global scale.

ENDNOTES

Too small? Read a larger print version at
www.nonobviousdiversity.com/resources

INTRODUCTION

1 TV 2 PLAY, "TV 2 | All That We Share," YouTube video, 3:00, January 27, 2017, https://www.youtube.com/watch?v=jD8tjhVO1Tc&ab_channel=TV2PLAY

CHAPTER 1

1 Reuters, "First Woman Competes at Middle East's Top Falconry Show," VOA News, last modified December 8, 2020, https://www.voanews.com/arts-culture/first-woman-competes-middle-easts-top-falconry-show

2 Reuters, "Rachael Blackmore makes history with Grand National win on Minella Times," ESPN, last modified April 10, 2021, https://www.espn.com/horse-racing/story/_/id/31229769/blackmore-makes-history-grand-national-win-minella-s

3 Myriam Gurba, "Pendeja, You Ain't Steinbeck: My Bronca with Fake-Ass Social Justice Literature," Topics of Meta, last modified December 12, 2019, https://tropicsofmeta.com/2019/12/12/pendeja-you-aint-steinbeck-my-bronca-with-fake-ass-social-justice-literature/

4 Barbara Vandenburgh, "Oprah's Book Club tackles controversial 'American Dirt' on Apple TV+ and it's super awkward," USA Today Entertainment, accessed July 21, 2021, https://eu.usatoday.com/story/entertainment/books/2020/03/06/oprah-winfreys-book-club-awkwardly-tackles-american-dirt/4972819002/

5 "What You See Isn't What You Get: The Role of Media in Anti-Asian Racism," Nielsen, last modified March 17, 2021, https://www.nielsen.com/us/en/insights/article/2021/what-you-see-isnt-what-you-get-the-role-of-media-in-anti-asian-racism/

6 Samuel Spencer, "'The Simpsons' New Season Is First with No White Actors in Non-White Roles," Newsweek, last modified September 27, 2020, https://www.newsweek.com/simpsons-season-32-non-white-characters-new-carl-1534315

7 Stacy L. Smith, Marc Choueiti, and Katherine Pieper, *Inequality in 1,300 Popular Films: Examining Portrayals of Gender, Race/Ethnicity, LGBTQ & Disability from 2007 to 2019* (USC Annenberg Inclusion Initiative and Annenberg Foundation, 2020).

8 Madeline Berg, "The Founder of America's Black Millennial Newsroom Speaks Out about Media Diversity," Forbes, last modified June 12, 2020, https://www.forbes.com/sites/maddieberg/2020/06/12/the-founder-of-americas-black-millennial-newsroom-speaks-out-about-media-diversity/?sh=4f66ce0e74ca

9 Ted Sarandos, "Building a Legacy of Inclusion: Results from Our First Film and Series Diversity Study," Netflix, last modified February 26, 2021, https://about.netflix.com/en/news/building-a-legacy-of-inclusion

10   Concepción de León and Elizabeth A. Harris, "#PublishingPaidMe and a Day of Action Reveal an Industry Reckoning," The New York Times, last modified June 10, 2020, https://www.nytimes.com/2020/06/08/books/publishingpaidme-publishing-day-of-action.html

11   Reggie Ugwu, "The Hashtag That Changed the Oscars: An Oral History," The New York Times, last modified September 9, 2020, https://www.nytimes.com/2020/02/06/movies/oscarssowhite-history.html

12   "Scientists can see the bias in your brain," Neuroscience News, last modified March 16, 2020, https://neurosciencenews.com/brain-bias-15922/

CHAPTER 2

1   Behind the Brand, "Seth Godin | One bit of advice that will change your life," YouTube video, 9:03, February 19, 2018, https://www.youtube.com/watch?v=YO-hnbbK_lc&ab_channel=BehindtheBrand

2   Elly Belle, "Now List 2021: Lydia X.Z. Brown's Advocacy Makes Space for Disabled People of Color," them, last modified June 28, 2021, https://www.them.us/story/now-list-2021-lydia-xz-brown/amp

3   Kristin Pauker et al., "The Role of Diversity Exposure in Whites' Reduction in Race Essentialism Over Time," Social Psychological and Personality Science 9, no. 8 (2018): 944- 52, https://doi.org/10.1177/1948550617731496

4   Beecher Reuning, "The Labels We Carry," Vimeo video, 2:30, https://vimeo.com/156164858

CHAPTER 3

1   Kristen Bialik, "Key facts about race and marriage, 50 years after Loving v. Virginia," Pew Research Center, last modified June 12, 2017, https://www.pewresearch.org/fact-tank/2017/06/12/key-facts-about-race-and-marriage-50-years-after-loving-v-virginia/

2   Sayaka Osanami Törngren, Nahikari Irastorza, and Dan Rodríguez-García, "Understanding multiethnic and multiracial experiences globally: towards a conceptual framework of mixedness," Journal of Ethnic and Migration Studies 47, no. 4 (2021): 763-81, https://www.diva-portal.org/smash/get/diva2:1398793/FULLTEXT01.pdf

3   Heidi Williams, "Stepfamilies around the world: How do we compare?," Oregon Live, last modified January 10, 2019, https://www.oregonlive.com/themombeat/2012/10/stepfamilies_around_the_world.html

4   Pew Research Center, Parenting in America: Outlook, worries, aspirations are strongly linked to financial situation (Pew Research Center, 2015), https://www.pewresearch.org/social-trends/2015/12/17/1-the-american-family-today/

5   Jordan Thierry, "In Praise of Black Fathers," Open Society Foundations, last modified June 15, 2011, https://www.opensocietyfoundations.org/voices/praise-black-fathers

6   Skye Schooley, "What Is Flextime, and Why Should You Offer It?," Business, last modified November 12, 2020, https://www.business.com/articles/advantages-of-flextime

CHAPTER 4

1   Courtney L. McCluney et al., "The Costs of Code-Switching," Harvard Business Review, last modified November 15, 2019, https://hbr.org/2019/11/the-costs-of-codeswitching

2   Gene Demby, "How Code-Switching Explains the World," NPR, last modified April 8, 2013, https://www.npr.org/sections/codeswitch/2013/04/08/176064688/how-code-switching-explains-the-world

3   Robin Lustig, "Can English remain the 'world's favourite' language?," BBC News, last modified May 23, 2018, https://www.bbc.co.uk/news/world-44200901

4   Stephen M. R. Covey and Douglas R. Conant, "The Connection Between Employee Trust and Financial Performance," Harvard Business Review, last modified July 18, 2016, https://hbr.org/2016/07/the-connection-between-employee-trust-and-financial-performance

CHAPTER 5

1 "The Poorest Children Are Four Times More Likely To Be Out of Primary School than the Richest Children," UNESCO, accessed July 21, 2021, https://en.unesco.org/gem-report/poorest-children-are-four-times-more-likely-be-out-primary-school-richest-children

2 John Komlos, "In America, inequality begins in the womb," PBS, last modified May 20, 2015, https://www.pbs.org/newshour/economy/making-sense/america-inequality-begins-womb

3 "Children Notice Race Several Years Before Adults Want to Talk About It," American Psychological Association, last modified August 27, 2020, https://www.apa.org/news/press/releases/2020/08/children-notice-race

4 Julie Brosnan, "New Zealand Is a Model of Cultural Education... We're Not," New America, last modified September 12, 2019, https://www.newamerica.org/weekly/new-zealand-model-cultural-education-were-not/

5 "Characteristics of Public School Teachers," National Center for Education Statistics, last modified May 2021, https://nces.ed.gov/programs/coe/indicator/clr

6 Grace Chen, "White Students are Now the Minority in U.S. Public Schools," *Public School Review* (blog), October 14, 2019, https://www.publicschoolreview.com/blog/white-students-are-now-the-minority-in-u-s-public-schools

7 Tim Walker, "Who is the Average U.S. Teacher?," NEA News, last modified August 6, 2018, https://www.nea.org/advocating-for-change/new-from-nea/who-average-us-teacher#:~:text=About%2077%20percent%20of%20public,84%20percent%20in%201999%2D2000.

CHAPTER 6

1 Tiffany Burns et al., "The diversity imperative in retail," McKinsey & Company, last modified January 13, 2021, https://www.mckinsey.com/industries/retail/our-insights/the-diversity-imperative-in-retail

2 Katie Oertli Mooney, "Groundbreaking Sephora Study Shows Racial Bias is Entrenched in the U.S. Retail Experience," Diversity Best Practices, last modified January 14, 2021, https://www.diversitybestpractices.com/groundbreaking-sephora-study-shows-racial-bias-is-entrenched-in-us-retail-experience

3 Rebecca Smithers, "Disabled shoppers deterred by difficult high street experience," The Guardian, last modified January 14, 2014, https://www.theguardian.com/money/2014/jan/14/disabled-shoppers-deterred-high-street-shop-online

4 Kathryn H. Anthony, "How Stores Are Designed to Fat Shame," Fast Company, last modified March 15, 2017, https://www.fastcompany.com/3068975/how-stores-are-designed-to-fat-shame

5 "Virtual reality continues to make people sick," The Economist, last modified November 23, 2019, https://www.economist.com/science-and-technology/2019/11/23/virtual-reality-continues-to-make-people-sick

6 Johnny Lieu, "Supermarket brings in 'quiet hour' designed to help autistic people," Mashable, last modified August 17, 2017, https://mashable.com/2017/08/17/quiet-hour-autism-supermarket/#O0HDULBhTaqI

7 "Inside Target's Plans to Spend More Than $2 Billion with Black-Owned Businesses by 2025," Corporate Target, last modified April 7, 2021, https://corporate.target.com/article/2021/04/reach-guest-experience

8 Jonathan Ringen, "How Lego Became The Apple Of Toys," Fast Company, last modified August 1, 2015, https://www.fastcompany.com/3040223/when-it-clicks-it-clicks

9 "Harley Davidson Misfires With Female Riders," Times Square Investment Journal, accessed July 21, 2021, https://coveringcompanies.journalism.cuny.edu/2020/01/26/harley-davidson-misfires-with-female-riders/

10 Doug Stanglin, "Nike begins selling sports hijab for Muslim female athletes," USA Today News, accessed July 21, 2021, https://www.usatoday.com/story/news/world/2017/12/20/nike-begins-selling-sports-hijab-muslim-female-athletes/970226001/

11 Chauncey Alcorn, "How gay couples in TV commercials became a mainstream phenomenon," CNN Business, last modified December 20, 2019, https://www.cnn.com/2019/12/20/media/hallmark-zola-gay-ad/index.html

12 Alison McCarthy, "Do Ads with a Possible Liberal Spin Pose too Much Risk? Survey data suggests diversity appeals to many viewers," eMarketer, last modified February 7, 2017, https://www.emarketer.com/Article/Do-Ads-with-Possible-Liberal-Spin-Pose-too-Much-Risk/1015187

CHAPTER 7

1 Jennifer Brown, "Unlocking the Potential of Neurodiverse Talent with Dr. Dave Caudel," May 22, 2020, *Jennifer Brown Speaks,* podcast, MP3 audio, 01:06:50, https://jenniferbrownspeaks. com/2020/05/22/unlocking-the-potential-of-neurodiverse-talent-with-dr-dave-caudel/

2 The Associated Press, "Europe seeks disabled astronauts, more women in space," ABC News, last modified June 23, 2021, https://abcnews.go.com/Technology/wireStory/europe-seeks-disabled-astronauts-women-space-78438228

3 Adia H. Robinson, "Starbucks Opens Its First 'Signing Store' For the Deaf and Hard of Hearing in DC Today," Washingtonian, last modified October 23, 2018, https://www.washingtonian. com/2018/10/23/starbucks-opens-its-first-signing-store-for-the-deaf-and-hard-of-hearing-in-dc/

4 Business Solver, "2020 State of Workplace Empathy," Business Solver, 2020, https://www.businessolver.com/workplace-empathy-executive-summary

CHAPTER 8

1 William Gallagher, "One year later, the Apple Card is a huge but controversial success," appleinsider, last modified August 20, 2020, https://appleinsider.com/articles/20/08/20/one-year-later-the-apple-card-is-a-huge-but-controversial-success

2 Ziad Obermeyer et al., "Dissecting racial bias in an algorithm used to manage the health of populations," *Science* 366, no. 6464 (2019): 447-453, https://science.sciencemag.org/content/366/6464/447.abstract

3 Caroline Criado-Perez, "The deadly truth about a world built for men – from stab vests to car crashes," The Guardian, last modified February 13, 2019, https://www.theguardian.com/lifeandstyle/2019/feb/23/truth-world-built-for-men-car-crashes

4 Terence Shin, "Real-life Examples of Discriminating Artificial Intelligence," Towards Data Science, last modified June 4, 2020, https://towardsdatascience.com/real-life-examples-of-discriminating-artificial-intelligence-cae395a90070

5 Joy Buolamwini, "The Algorithmic Justice League," MIT Media Lab, last modified December 15, 2016, https://medium.com/mit-media-lab/the-algorithmic-justice-league-3cc4131c5148

6 The Algorithmic Justice League, *The Algorithmic Justice League's 101 Overview* (The Algorithmic Justice League, 2020), https://www.ajl.org/learn-more

7 Deborah Raji, "How our data encodes systematic racism," Technology Review, last modified December 10, 2020, https://www.technologyreview.com/2020/12/10/1013617/racism-data-science-artificial-intelligence-ai-opinion/

8 Isis Anchalee, "You May Have Seen My Face on BART," The Coffeelicious, last modified August 1, 2015, https://medium.com/the-coffeelicious/you-may-have-seen-my-face-on-bart-8b9561003e0f

9 Galen Gruman, "The state of ethnic minorities in U.S. tech: 2020," Computerworld, last modified September 21, 2020, https://www.computerworld.com/article/3574917/the-state-of-ethnic-minorities-in-us-tech-2020.html

10 Conor Cawley, "Study: Tech Giants Are Getting Worse at Promoting Equal Pay," Tech.co, last modified March 21, 2021, https://tech.co/news/study-tech-giants-equal-pay

11 Isis Anchalee, "New Chapters: Why I'm Leaving Silicon Valley," Making Love With Life, last modified January 22, 2019, https://makinglovewith.wpcomstaging.com/2019/01/22/%E2%9D%82-new-chapters-why-im-leaving-silicon-valley/

12 "The Fallout of Wage Gaps," Hiredpod, accessed July 21, 2021, https://hiredprod.wpengine.com/h/wage-inequality-report/2020/#fallout

13 Sigal Samuel, "10 things we should all demand from Big Tech right now," Vox, last modified May 29, 2019, https://www.vox.com/the-highlight/2019/5/22/18273284/ai-algorithmic-bill-of-rights-accountability-transparency-consent-bias

CHAPTER 9

1 Peter Vandor and Nikolaus Franke, "Why Are Immigrants More Entrepreneurial?," Harvard Business Review, last modified October 27, 2016, https://hbr.org/2016/10/why-are-immigrants-more-entrepreneurial

2 Peter Vandor and Nikolaus Franke, "Why Are Immigrants More Entrepreneurial?," Harvard Business Review, last modified October 27, 2016, https://hbr.org/2016/10/why-are-immi-

grants-more-entrepreneurial

3 Johnny Wood, "Immigrants make good entrepreneurs. This study proves it," World Economic Forum, last modified November 2, 2018, https://www.weforum.org/agenda/2018/11/immigrants-make-good-entrepreneurs-this-study-proves-it/

4 Dan Kosten, "Immigrants as Economic Contributors: Immigrant Entrepreneurs," National Immigration Forum, last modified July 11, 2018, https://immigrationforum.org/article/immigrants-as-economic-contributors-immigrant-entrepreneurs/

5 "Global Press Release," Global Entrepreneurship Monitor, accessed July 21, 2021, https://www.gemconsortium.org/reports/latest-global-report

6 Brittany Cronin and Cardiff Garcia, "Entrepreneurship On The Rise," NPR, last modified January 11, 2021, https://www.npr.org/2021/01/11/955697672/entrepreneurship-on-the-rise

7 Hayley Leibson, "The Secret Lives Of Entrepreneurs Revealed," Forbes, last modified October 31, 2018, https://www.forbes.com/sites/hayleyleibson/2018/10/31/the-secret-lives-of-entrepreneurs-revealed/#27fabb0236ca

8 "Persons with a Disability: Labor Force Characteristics Summary," U.S. Bureau of Labor Statistics, last modified February 24, 2021, https://www.bls.gov/news.release/disabl.nr0.htm

9 "Research: Women Entrepreneurs Reverse the Gender Pay Gap," Glass Ceiling, accessed July 21, 2021, http://glassceiling.com/research-women-entrepreneurs-reverse-gender-pay-gap/

10 "10 Year Project," First Round, accessed July 21, 2021, http://10years.firstround.com/

11 Lisa Stone, "Diversity As $uperpower: The (Well-Known) Data Against Homogeneous Teams In Venture Capital," last modified September 22, 2020, https://www.forbes.com/sites/committeeof200/2020/09/22/diversity-as-uperpower-the-well-known-data-against-homogeneous-teams-in-venture-capital/?sh=37c5657d2019

12 Lisa Stone, "Diversity As $uperpower: The (Well-Known) Data Against Homogeneous Teams In Venture Capital," last modified September 22, 2020, https://www.forbes.com/sites/committeeof200/2020/09/22/diversity-as-uperpower-the-well-known-data-against-homogeneous-teams-in-venture-capital/?sh=4db910e92019

13 Lisa Stone, "Diversity As $uperpower: The (Well-Known) Data Against Homogeneous Teams In Venture Capital," last modified September 22, 2020, https://www.forbes.com/sites/committeeof200/2020/09/22/diversity-as-uperpower-the-well-known-data-against-homogeneous-teams-in-venture-capital/?sh=4db910e92019

CHAPTER 10

1 "The state of women in corporate America," Lean In, accessed July 21, 2021, https://leanin.org/women-in-the-workplace-2019?

2 "Women and Minorities on Fortune 500 Boards: More Room to Grow," The Wall Street Journal, accessed July 21, 2021, https://deloitte.wsj.com/riskandcompliance/2019/03/12/women-and-minorities-on-fortune-500-boards-more-room-to-grow/

3 "Women in Management (Quick Take)," Catalyst, last modified August 11, 2020, https://www.catalyst.org/research/women-in-management/

4 Michelle K. Ryan and S. Alexander Haslam, "The Glass Cliff: Exploring the Dynamics Surrounding the Appointment of Women to Precarious Leadership Positions," The Academy of Management Review 32, no. 2 (2007): 549- 572, https://www.jstor.org/stable/20159315?seq=1#metadata_info_tab_contents

5 Guy Caruso and Kathy Miller, "Board Diversity Includes Disabilities," BoardSource (blog), October 25, 2019, https://blog.boardsource.org/blog/board-diversity-includes-disabilities

CHAPTER 11

1 Christopher Ingraham, "About 100 million people couldn't be bothered to vote this year," The Washington Post, last modified November 12, 2016, https://www.washingtonpost.com/news/wonk/wp/2016/11/12/about-100-million-people-couldnt-be-bothered-to-vote-this-year/

2 Christy Mallory, The 2020 LGBT Vote Preferences and Characteristics of LGBT Voters (Los Angeles: UCLA School of Law, Williams Institute, 2019), https://williamsinstitute.law.ucla.edu/publications/the-2020-lgbt-vote/?mod=article_inline

3 Reflective Democracy Campaign, Confronting the Demographics of Power: America's Cities 2020 (Women Donors Network, 2020), https://wholeads.us/research/americas-cities-data/

4 "Out for America 2020," Victory Institute, accessed July 21, 2021, https://victoryinstitute.org/out-for-america-2020/
5 Renuka Rayasam et al., "Why state legislatures are still very white — and very male," Politico, last modified February 23, 2021, https://www.politico.com/interactives/2021/state-legislature-demographics/
6 Salimah Shivji, "Five years on, Trudeau's vow to build a diverse public service still unfulfilled," CBC News, last modified June 12, 2020, https://www.cbc.ca/news/politics/diversity-public-service-trudeau-1.5607977
7 Amanda Taub, "Why Are Women-Led Nations Doing Better With Covid-19?," The New York Times, last modified Aug 13, 2020, https://www.nytimes.com/2020/05/15/world/coronavirus-women-leaders.html
8 Rachel B. Vogelstein and Alexandra Bro, "Women's Power Index," Council on Foreign Relations, last modified March 29, 2021, https://www.cfr.org/article/womens-power-index
9 Jamie Smyth, "Jacinda Ardern appoints most diverse cabinet in New Zealand history," Financial Times, last modified November 2, 2020, https://www.ft.com/content/ccfc8195-aa97-4845-b16b-4f0762a168ed
10 Abdurashid Solijonov, *Voter Turnout Trends around the World* (Strömsborg: International IDEA, 2016), https://www.idea.int/sites/default/files/publications/voter-turnout-trends-around-the-world.pdf
11 Richard Wike and Alexandra Castillo, "Many Around the World Are Disengaged From Politics," Pew Research Center, last modified October 17, 2018, https://www.pewresearch.org/global/2018/10/17/international-political-engagement/
12 Pamela Ban, Elena Llaudet, and James M. Snyder, "Challenger Quality and the Incumbency Advantage," Legislative Studies Quarterly 41, no. 1 (2016):153-179, https://scholar.harvard.edu/files/ellaudet/files/challenger_quality_and_the_incumbency_advantage.pdf
13 Grace Panetta, "How Black Americans still face disproportionate barriers to the ballot box in 2020," Insider, last modified September 18, 2020, https://www.businessinsider.com/why-black-americans-still-face-obstacles-to-voting-at-every-step-2020-6
14 Asian Americans Advancing Justice, accessed July 21, 2021, https://www.advancingjustice-aajc.org/
15 Nicholas Kristof, "How Can You Hate Me When You Don't Even Know Me," The New York Times, last modified June 26, 2021, https://www.nytimes.com/2021/06/26/opinion/racism-politics-daryl-davis.html

CHAPTER 12

1 Rose Eveleth, "Why Aren't There More Women Futurists?," The Atlantic, last modified July 31, 2015, https://www.theatlantic.com/technology/archive/2015/07/futurism-sexism-men/400097/
2 "Dorceta Taylor," Yale School of Environment, accessed July 21, 2021, https://environment.yale.edu/profile/taylor
3 Xiye Bastida, "My name is not Greta Thunberg: Why diverse voices matter in the climate movement," The Elders, last modified June 19, 2020, https://theelders.org/news/my-name-not-greta-thunberg-why-diverse-voices-matter-climate-movement
4 Oscar Perry Abello, "Breaking Through and Breaking Down the Delmar Divide in St. Louis," Next City, last modified August 19, 2019, https://nextcity.org/features/view/breaking-through-and-breaking-down-the-delmar-divide-in-st.-louis
5 Katrina Johnston-Zimmerman, "Urban Planning Has a Sexism Problem," Next City, last modified December 19, 2017, https://nextcity.org/features/view/urban-planning-sexism-problem
6 Clare Foran, "How to Design a City for Women: A fascinating experiment in "gender mainstreaming," Bloomberg CityLab, last modified September 16, 2013, https://www.bloomberg.com/news/articles/2013-09-16/how-to-design-a-city-for-women
7 Martha Chen and Victoria A. Beard, "Including the Excluded: Supporting Informal Workers for More Equal and Productive Cities in the Global South," World Resources Report Working Paper, World Resources Institute, Washington, 2018, https://www.wri.org/wri-citiesforall/publication/including-the-excluded
8 "Our Work: Urban Design," Asiye eTafuleni, accessed July 21, 2021, https://aet.org.za/what-we-do/inclusive-design/
9 C. Brandon Ogbunu, "How Afrofuturism Can Help the World Mend," Wired, last modified July 15, 2020, https://www.wired.com/story/how-afrofuturism-can-help-the-world-mend/

INDEX